PEGASUS ENCYCLOPEDIA LIBRARY

Food and Nutrition
DIET AND RECIPES

Edited by: Pallabi B. Tomar, Hitesh Iplani
Managing editor: Tapasi De
Designed by: Vijesh Chahal, Anil Kumar, Rohit Kumar
Illustrated by: Suman S. Roy, Tanoy Choudhury
Colouring done by: Vinay Kumar, Kiran Kumari & Pradeep Kumar

DIET AND RECIPES

CONTENTS

Introduction 3

Balanced diet 5

Types of diets 7

Body mass index 11

Importance of diet 13

Role of nutrients 15

Diet according to body types 18

Some healthy recipes 21

Test Your Memory 31

Index 32

Introduction

Diet is the sum of food consumed by a person or other living being. The human body is a large and complicated organism. There are many different parts of the body that perform several unique functions. Different organ systems perform automatic tasks that help maintain the life of the body. This complicated nature of the human body means that its dietary requirements are equally complicated. A healthy diet is therefore one that contains all the necessary nutrients in appropriate amounts. The dietary requirement of every human being is different from every other human being. Some individuals are more athletic and spend more energy while others are more relaxed and tend not to spend too much time on physical pursuits. The profession of an individual is also important when it comes to a balanced diet. Some individuals' work involves intense physical labour, while others sit at desks all day and do not expend much physical energy. Instead, these people spend their energy on mental tasks. Therefore, a lumberjack working in a forest requires a different diet from that of an IT professional working in an office.

In general, raw vegetables have a much higher nutrient value than cooked, though there are a few exceptions, such as cooked tomatoes.

DIET AND RECIPES

The human body requires food to provide energy for all life process and for growth, repair and maintenance of cells and tissues. The dietetic needs vary according to age, sex and occupation. A balanced diet contains different types of foods in such quantities and proportions that the need for calories, minerals, vitamins and other nutrients is adequately met. A small provision is also made of extra nutrients which the body might need to fall back on short periods of leanness. Eating a well balanced diet on a regular basis and maintaining your ideal weight are critical factors in maintaining your emotional and physical well-being. Being over weight/under weight can lead to certain chronic conditions such as diabetes, high blood pressure and heart disease.

Fluid intake in the form of water based drinks is also essential for good health. Water is essential for the correct functioning of the kidneys and bowels. At least 6-8 glasses of plain water should be drunk each day, more in hot weather.

Astonishing fact

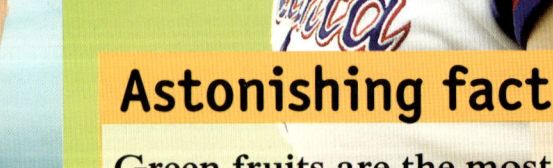

Green fruits are the most vital of all fruits since they contain a chemical that protects you against heart attack and keeps your heart healthy.

Balanced diet

A balanced diet is one that has all the essential nutrients, required by the body for proper growth and development, in the appropriate amounts. A well balanced diet consists of the right amounts of carbohydrates, proteins, fats, vitamins and minerals. A balanced diet also provides the body energy to function.

A balanced diet is one that features foods from all the important food groups that are used by the human body. These food groups include **protein** which is used to build body tissue, **carbohydrates** that are used for energy, **vitamins** and **minerals** that are used for various important body functions, **fat** that is used for energy storage and dietary fibre which helps the process of digestion.

When choosing a healthy diet, one should focus on naturally occurring foods rather than processed foods. All natural foods have varied nutritional qualities. Processed foods maybe rich in certain nutrients, but may fall short in other areas. A natural food based diet is one that can be a healthy diet and a balanced diet as well. A good, nutritious diet is essential for the proper functioning of the body and the proper functioning of the mind as well. When the body is in harmony, the individual can perform his or her daily tasks more efficiently.

The mega-sized apples and oranges seen at grocers are pumped up due to added water volume, rather than fruit substance. This is a crop-yield technique used by farmers designed to produce bigger fruit for more consumer appeal.

5

DIET AND RECIPES

When it comes to a diet for weight loss, one should understand that there are two areas of focus. Firstly, weight loss is related to the amount of exercise that an individual does. During exercise, food and then fat is burned for energy. By reducing one's food consumption, one will only achieve partial results. Starving the body is not a good plan as this causes sudden weight loss and may result in some sort of toxicity within the body, especially if there is no balance in the system. The second aspect of a diet for weight loss is the quantity and quality of food that is consumed. Once an individual has a set exercise regime, the diet can be modified accordingly. Individuals should eat meals at a set time and should avoid irregular snacking. Exercise should be done in an empty stomach so that the body needs to access fat for energy much faster than it would on a full stomach. An extensive use of fruits and vegetables is recommended.

A diet for weight loss and muscle gain is based on higher protein than a normal healthy diet. This is because protein is the raw material that is used to build muscle tissue.

> **Astonishing fact**
>
> The flavour of bubble gum comes from the fusion of vanilla, wintergreen and 'cassia,' a form of cinnamon.

Types of diets

Fixed-menu diet

A fixed-menu diet provides a list of all the foods you will eat. This kind of diet can be easy to follow because the foods are selected for you. But you get very few different food choices which may make the diet boring and hard to follow. In addition, fixed-menu diets do not teach the food selection skills necessary for keeping weight off. If you start with a fixed-menu diet, you should switch eventually to a plan that helps you learn to make meal choices on your own, such as an exchange-type diet.

Exchange-type diet

An exchange-type diet is a meal plan with a set number of servings from each of several food groups. Within each group, foods are about equal in calories and can be interchanged as you wish. For example,

the 'starch' category could include one slice of bread or 1/2 cup of oatmeal; each is about equal in nutritional value and calories. If your meal plan calls for two starch choices at breakfast, you could choose to eat two slices of bread, or one slice of bread and 1/2 cup of oatmeal. With the exchange-type diet plans, you have more day-to-day variety and you can easily follow the diet away from home. The most important advantage is that exchange-type diet plans teach the food selection skills you need to keep your weight off.

Astonishing fact

There is evidence that honey is the only food that does not spoil at all. Archaeologists have tasted honey discovered in ancient Egyptian tombs, reporting that it was still edible!

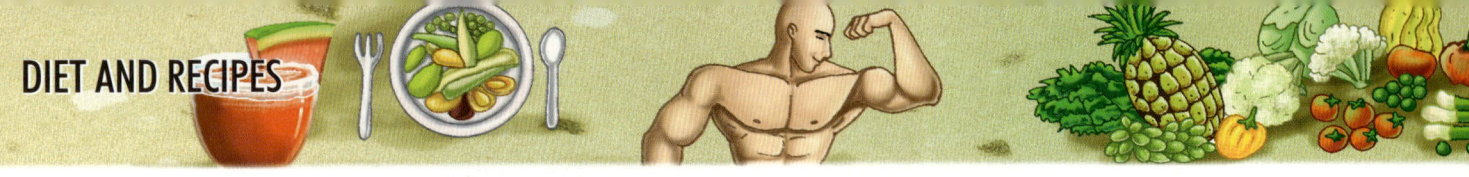

DIET AND RECIPES

Formula diet

Formula diets are weight-loss plans that replace one or more meals with a liquid formula. Most formula diets are balanced diets containing a mix of protein, carbohydrate and usually a small amount of fat. Formula diets are usually sold as liquid or a powder to be mixed with liquid. Although formula diets are easy to use and do promote short-term weight loss, most people regain the weight as soon as they stop using the formula. In addition, formula diets do not teach you how to make healthy food choices, a necessary skill for keeping your weight off.

Pre-packaged meal diet

These diets require you to buy pre-packaged meals. Such meals may help you learn appropriate portion sizes. However, they can be costly. Before beginning this type of program, find out whether you need to buy the meals or not and how much the meals would cost you. You should also find out whether the program will teach you how to select and prepare food, skills that are needed to sustain weight loss.

Astonishing fact

Popcorn have existed for around 6,000 years!

8

Types of diets

Questionable diets

You should avoid any diet that suggests you to eat a certain nutrient, food or combination of foods to promote easy weight loss. Some of these diets may work in the short term because they are low in calories. However, they are often not well balanced and may cause nutrient deficiencies. In addition, they do not teach eating habits that are important for a long-term weight management.

Flexible diets

Some programs or books suggest monitoring the fat only, calories only or a combination of the two, with the individual making the choice of both the type and amount of food eaten. This flexible type of approach works well for many people, and teach them how to control what they eat. One drawback of flexible diets is that some don't consider the total diet. For example, programs that monitor fat only often allow people to take in unlimited amounts of excess calories from sugars, and therefore don't lead to weight loss.

It is important to choose an eating plan that you can live with. The plan should also teach you how to select and prepare healthy foods, as well as how to maintain your new weight. Remember that many people tend to regain lost weight. Eating a healthful and nutritious diet to maintain your new weight, combined with regular physical activity, helps to prevent weight regain.

> **Astonishing fact**
>
> There are 1,200 varieties of watermelon.

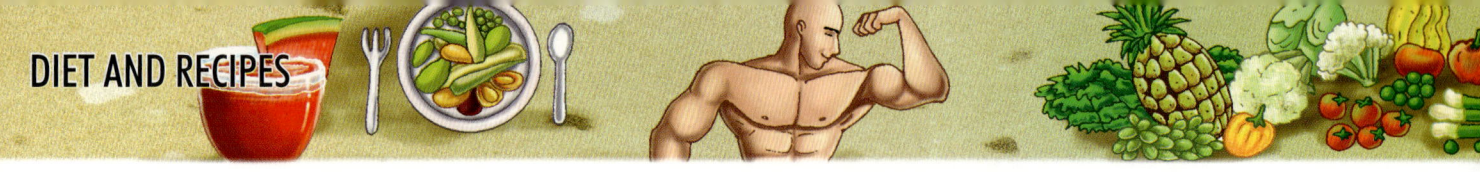

DIET AND RECIPES

Low-calorie diet

A low-calorie diet is a low-energy diet. The goal of a low-calorie diet is to create an energy deficit by providing fewer calories than your body needs so that the body has to draw upon the energy stored in body fat.

A low-calorie diet can be recognized by the types of foods recommended and the way they are prepared. Fresh fruits and vegetables, whole-grain cereals and breads, non-fat milk, yogurt, and other dairy products and lean meats, poultry, fish, and beans make up the bulk of the menu. Foods are prepared using low-calorie cooking methods. For example, meats, poultry and fish are roasted, baked or broiled, not fried. Vegetables are steamed, boiled or micro waved without using butter.

Low-fat diet

A low-fat diet is made up primarily of foods that contain carbohydrates and fibre, including whole-grain breads and cereals, fruits, vegetables, and dried beans and peas. A low-fat diet should contain fewer foods from animal sources or should replace them with foods that are low in fat like low-fat milk and yogurt.

In addition, a low-fat diet should contain more foods from plant sources, which provide fibre, are low in saturated fat, and do not contain cholesterol. Lean meats, poultry, fish and low-fat or non-fat milk and yogurt supply protein.

Astonishing fact

In order to have a therapeutic effect from green tea, you must consume 4-5 cups of it daily.

Body mass index

> The closer a food is to its natural state, the healthier it is for you. An apple is better than apple sauce which is better than bottled apple juice which is again better than apple pie.

Body mass index

Body mass index (BMI) is a calculation that uses your height and weight to estimate how much body fat you have. Too much body fat is a problem because it can lead to illnesses and other health problems. BMI, although not a perfect method for judging someone's weight, is often a good way to check on how a kid is growing.

The Body mass index (BMI) formula was developed by Belgium statistician Adolphe Quetelet (1796-1874) and was known as the Quetelet Index. BMI is also referred to as 'body mass indicator'. BMI is an internationally used measure of obesity.

BMI has been used by the World Health Organisation (WHO) as the standard for recording obesity statistics since the early 1980s. In the United States, BMI is also used as a measure of underweight.

DIET AND RECIPES

Body mass index calculation is very straightforward. Calculating body mass index requires only two measurements, height and weight.

The metric BMI formula accepts weight measurements in kilograms and height measurements in either centimetres or metres.

1 metre = 100 cms

metre² = metres × metres

Table: Metric BMI formula

$$BMI\ (kg/m^2) = \frac{\text{weight in kilograms}}{\text{height in metres}^2}$$

The formula is designed for adults over 20 years old. Once calculated, Body Mass Index can be compared to weight status categories to determine if an individual is:

- underweight (BMI: below 19.5)
- normal weight (BMI: 18.5 - 24.9)
- overweight (BMI: 25.0 to 29.9)
- obese (BMI: 30.0 & above)

> The reason some canned juices taste so good is because they contain a lot of sugar.

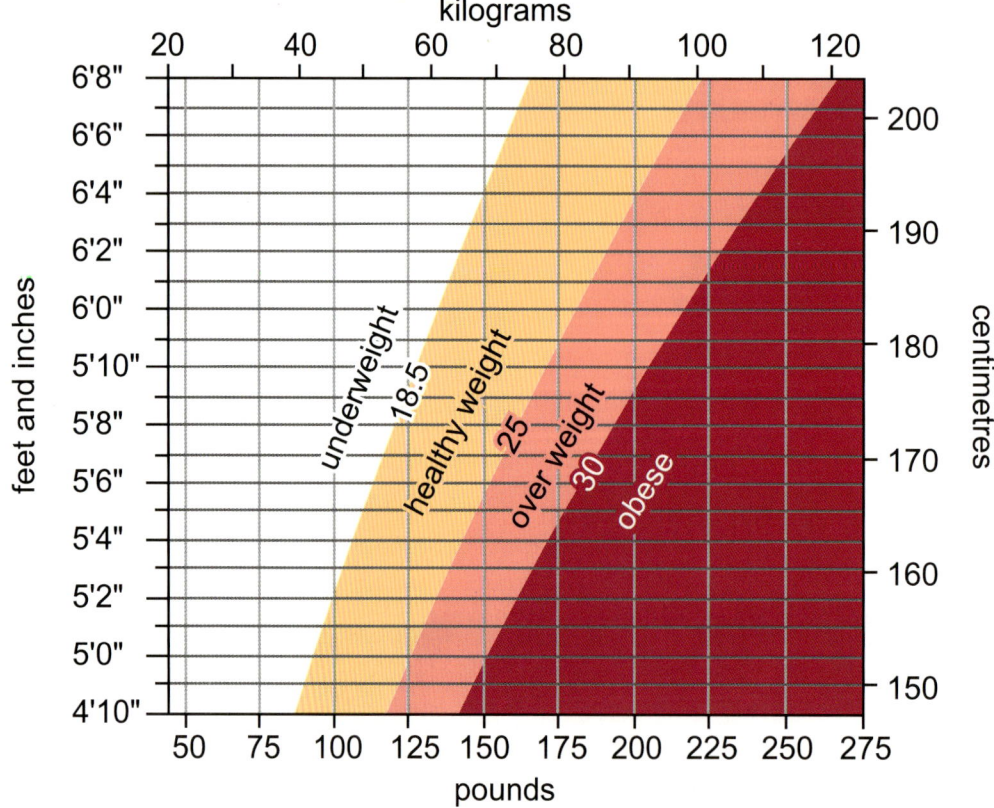

Body Mass Index (BMI) for adults

Source: National Institutes of Health/National Heart, Lung, and Blood Institute

Importance of diet

Nowadays, there are many health problems that people are experiencing, which are arising due to several reasons. For most of the problems, the correct and only solution is a balanced diet. Many people have a misconception that a balanced diet means to avoid eating specific foodstuffs which may prove harmful to the body. It actually means to eat all types of food, but in a balanced amount which will provide all necessary nutrients to maintain a healthy body.

Preventing infections and diseases

Eating all kinds of foods in a well-balanced proportion will help your body to prevent many infections and disorders. If the body gets all the required nutrients, it will improve the functioning of the immune system which is responsible for the prevention of various infections. By following a balanced diet, you reduce the possibilities of some types of cancer, control blood sugar levels effectively and control blood pressure also.

Controlling weight

For the purpose of reducing and controlling weight, people tend to forget why a balanced diet is important. They don't understand that a balanced diet is the key to reduce or increase weight. Those who want to reduce weight try different ways, but don't succeed. The reason is that the routines they choose include consuming huge amounts of foods that don't contribute to weight loss.

Astonishing fact

Bananas will never become brown, if you refrigerate them.

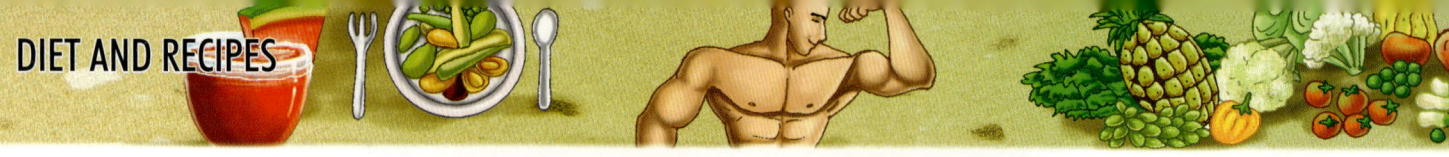

Healthy growth of a body

If the body is getting all the essential nutrients regularly, it will certainly be fit. It would be away from infections and diseases, which in turn will promote a healthy body, growth and maintenance. A balanced diet should be implemented in the routine of a growing child or a teenager. You would be able to easily perform physical tasks without any exertion on the body. It is a necessity nowadays, as there is so much physical and mental stress in the lives of people.

Active lifestyle

A balanced diet would also be beneficial to the state of mind. You would be able to live an active lifestyle. As both the body and mind would be in a good state, they would coordinate effectively. It will help you to take immediate decisions and tackle problems efficiently. It is also proven to increase the remembering and memorizing capability of a person.

There are many more advantages that a balanced diet has to offer. The chances of your body getting infected would be reduced considerably. It would also help you to stop the development and spreading of the diseases and infections which you are suffering from.

Role of nutrients

Our body needs important nutrients to support its healthy condition. It is mandatory that our food consumption should include healthy foods that contain good amount of nutrients sufficient enough to supply our body with its required daily nutrition.

Carbohydrates

Carbohydrates are the most important source of energy. They contain the elements carbon, hydrogen and oxygen. We obtain most of our carbohydrate in the form of starch. This is found in potato, rice, spaghetti, yams, bread and cereals. Our digestive system turns all this starch into another carbohydrate called **glucose**. Glucose is carried around the body in the blood and is used by our tissues as a source of energy. We also get some of our carbohydrate in the form of sucrose; this is the sugar which we put in our tea and coffee.

Proteins

Proteins are required for growth and repair. Where carbohydrates and fats are broken down to produce energy, protein is broken down to give your body material for tissue repair and growth. Common protein rich foods may include milk, soy milk, eggs, cheese, yogurt, peanut butter, lean meats, fish and poultry, beans, tofu, lentils and other legumes, grains, including bread and pasta, nuts and seeds.

Astonishing fact

Two 12-ounce servings of freshly juiced apples, pears, carrots, celery and leafy greens can produce the same effect as twice the dose of a laxative.

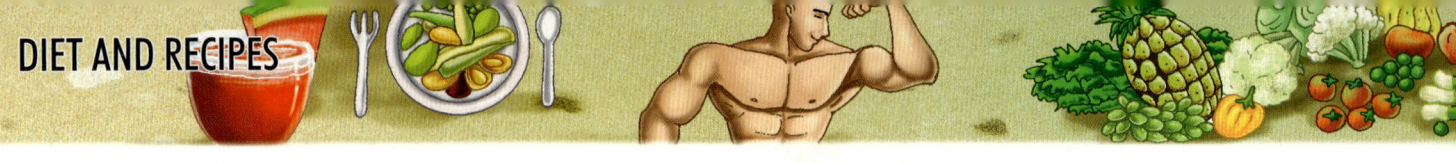

Fats

Fats are our storehouses of energy. When we have excess nutrients in our body, some of it is stored as fat. The primary purpose of fat is energy production. There are two main types of fats— saturated and unsaturated. Animal fats (meat, butter, lard) are usually saturated fats and contribute to heart disease and cancer. Vegetable fats (olive oil, corn oil) are generally unsaturated fats and are less harmful.

Vitamins

Vitamins are substances that your body needs to grow and develop normally. There are 13 vitamins your body needs. They are vitamins A, C, D, E, K and the B vitamins (thiamine, riboflavin, niacin, pantothenic acid, biotin, vitamin B-6, vitamin B-12 and folate). You can usually get all your vitamins from the foods you eat. Your body can also make vitamins D and K.

Each vitamin has specific jobs. If you have low levels of certain vitamins, you may develop a deficiency disease. For example, if you don't get enough vitamin D, you could develop rickets. Some vitamins may help prevent medical problems. Vitamin A prevents night blindness.

Astonishing fact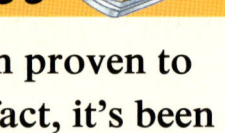

Diet soda has not been proven to aid in weight loss. In fact, it's been shown to actually increase hunger!

Role of nutrients

Minerals

Minerals are compounds obtained from your diet that combine in several ways to form the structures of your body. For instance, calcium is a mineral that is crucial in the formation and maintenance of your bones. Minerals also help regulate body functions. Minerals do not produce energy.

Water

Water is perhaps the most critical nutrient. We can live without other nutrients for several weeks, but we can go without water for only about one week. The body needs water to carry out all of its life processes. Watery solutions help dissolve other nutrients and carry them to all the tissues. The chemical reactions that turn food into energy or tissue-building materials can take place only in a watery solution. The body also needs water to carry away waste products and to cool itself.

> Whenever a recipe for cake or muffins calls for oil, applesauce can be substituted in place of it.

17

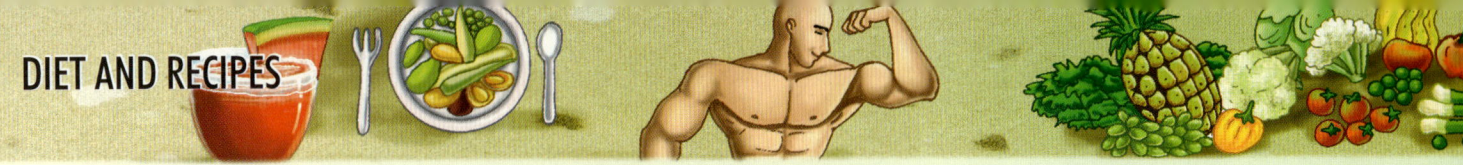

DIET AND RECIPES

Diet according to body types

All people fall into three basic body types— ectomorph, mesomorph and endomorph. A body type diet suggests that we eat certain foods based on our body type, and that eating this way will help promote a proper weight and our overall health and well-being.

Ectomorph body type diet

The ectomorph body type is naturally lean. If you are an ectomorph you will tend to be taller and tend to burn calories quickly. You may find it difficult to keep the weight on. This does not mean an ectomorph should indulge in greasy overly fatty foods. Doing so will only increase their risk of cardiovascular disease and high blood pressure, whether they are naturally lean or not. Rather an ectomorph should focus on eating multiple times per day and eating nutritious and calorie dense foods. Ample proteins, carbohydrates and fats should be included in the diet. Extra protein may help build more lean muscle.

Astonishing fact

Apples are more efficient than coffee at keeping people awake in the morning.

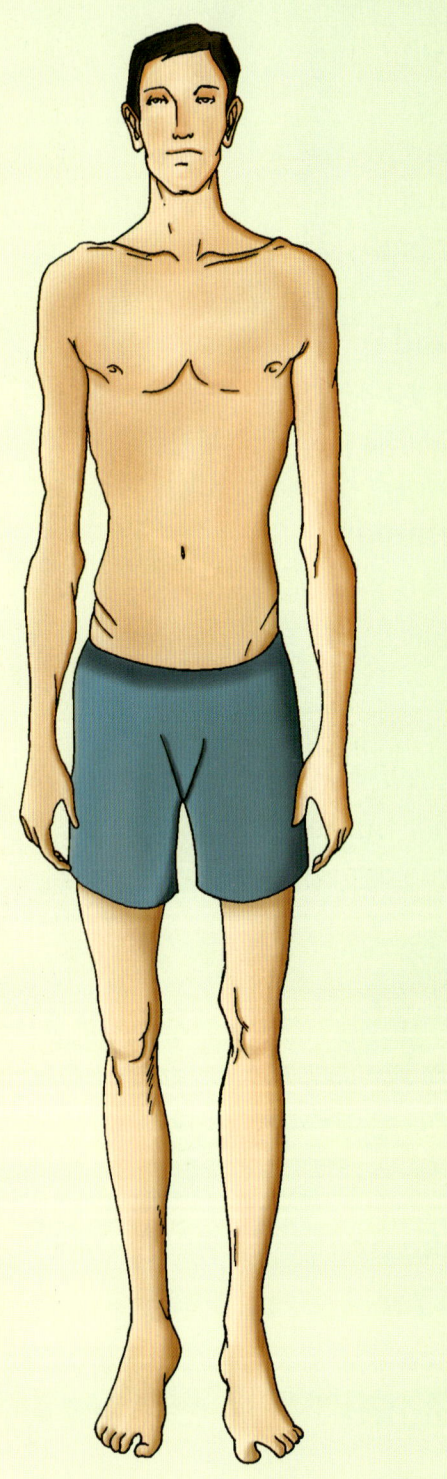
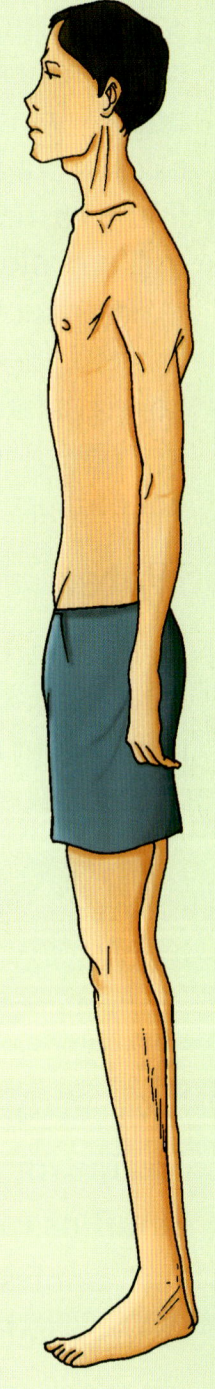

Mesomorph body type diet

People with a mesomorph body type have average builds with the muscle definition and strength of an athlete having broad shoulders and a narrow waist. Mesomorphs build muscle easily. A fast metabolism helps people with the mesomorph body type to lose fat and maintain weight when they follow a healthy diet and exercise program. Mesomorphs are more muscular than the endomorph or ectomorph body types.

Mesomorph metabolism is faster than the metabolism of the endomorph body type but slower than the metabolism of an ectomorph. It is easy for people with a mesomorph body type to lose excess weight when they follow a low-fat, high-protein eating plan with the proper number of calories and plenty of exercise. Mesomorphs gain weight quickly if their eating plans contain too many calories from high-fat, high-sugar foods. As mesomorphs age, they will need to follow a strict plan of diet and exercise to maintain their muscle mass and fitness level. Mesomorphs must be sure not to take their body type for granted or they will become fat and unfit.

Muscle building comes very easily to people with a mesomorph body type. This might be one of the reasons why so many professional athletes have this build. Even an out-of-shape mesomorph who wants to get back into shape will quickly change flabby muscles to fit, well-defined muscles with relative ease. Mesomorphs are solidly built and well-suited to activities that require strength and endurance, such as swimming and hiking.

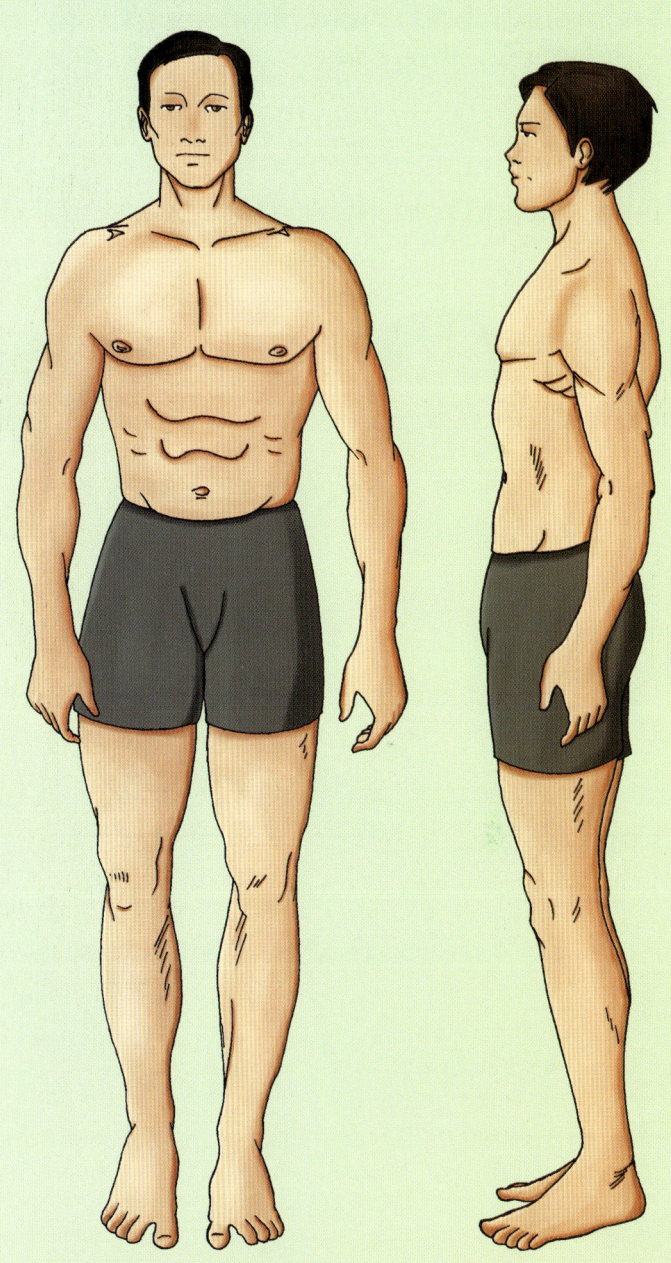

Astonishing fact
There are 15,000 different kinds of rice!

Diet and Recipes

Endomorph body type diet

The characteristics of an endomorph body type include a rounder body with a waist that is often bigger than the chest. Endomorph body types often have short arms and legs, with the upper part of the limbs being larger than the lower part. People with this body type tend to store fat easily and have more difficulty losing weight.

The endomorph body type maybe the hardest body type to have in terms of managing weight and overall fitness. The ectomorph body type usually describes people who are tall and skinny. The mesomorph body type describes people with an athletic body. A person with an endomorph body type usually has a slow metabolism. They eat small amounts of food and still tend to gain weight. Excess calories can turn into fat quickly for someone with an endomorph body type. It is possible for endomorphs to lose weight, but it can sometimes be a slow process.

Those with an endomorph body type need to stay on a strict diet in order to maintain a healthy weight and lifestyle. This body type does not process carbohydrates well. Endomorphs should eat a diet of low carbohydrates and consume plenty of protein. Protein can help people with this body type gain muscle and burn fat.

Eating meals that are lower in fat will also help people with an endomorph body type. Some believe that endomorphs have more fat cells in the body than other body types. Low-fat meals and snacks will decrease the chance of creating more fat cells in the body. A low-fat diet should be filled with healthy foods such as lean meats, fruits and vegetables.

Astonishing fact

Rice is the chief food for half the people of the world.

Some healthy recipes

Buckwheat buttermilk pancakes

Ingredients

- 1 cup flour
- ½ teaspoon salt
- 1 teaspoon baking powder
- 1 teaspoon baking soda
- 2 tablespoons sugar
- 1 cup buckwheat flour
- 1 egg, well beaten
- ¼ cup butter, melted (or ¼ c. salad oil)
- 2 cups buttermilk

Method

Into a medium bowl, mix flour with salt, baking powder, baking soda and sugar. Stir in buckwheat flour. Set aside.

In another small bowl mix egg, butter and buttermilk well. Add to the flour mixture, mixing only until combined (will be lumpy).

In the meantime, slowly heat a griddle or frying pan. Use 1/4 cup batter for each pancake. Cook until bubbles form on surface and edges become dry. Turn; cook for 2 minutes longer or until nicely browned on underside. Serve warm, with butter and maple syrup.

Astonishing fact

After the 'Popeye' comic strip started in 1931; spinach consumption went up by thirty-three per cent in the United States!

DIET AND RECIPES

Western omelette

Ingredients

- 1/2 cup egg substitute
- 1/2 cup potatoes, diced
- 1/4 cup of finely chopped green peppers
- 1/4 cup of finely chopped red peppers
- 1/4 cup of finely chopped onions
- 1 teaspoon light margarine

Method

In a non-stick frying pan, over medium heat, fry potatoes, peppers and onions in 1-teaspoon light margarine until tender. Remove from frying pan; keep warm.

Pour egg substitute into frying pan. Cook lifting edges to allow uncooked portion to flow underneath.

When almost set, spoon vegetable mixture over half of the omelette. Fold other half over vegetable mixture; slide onto serving plate.

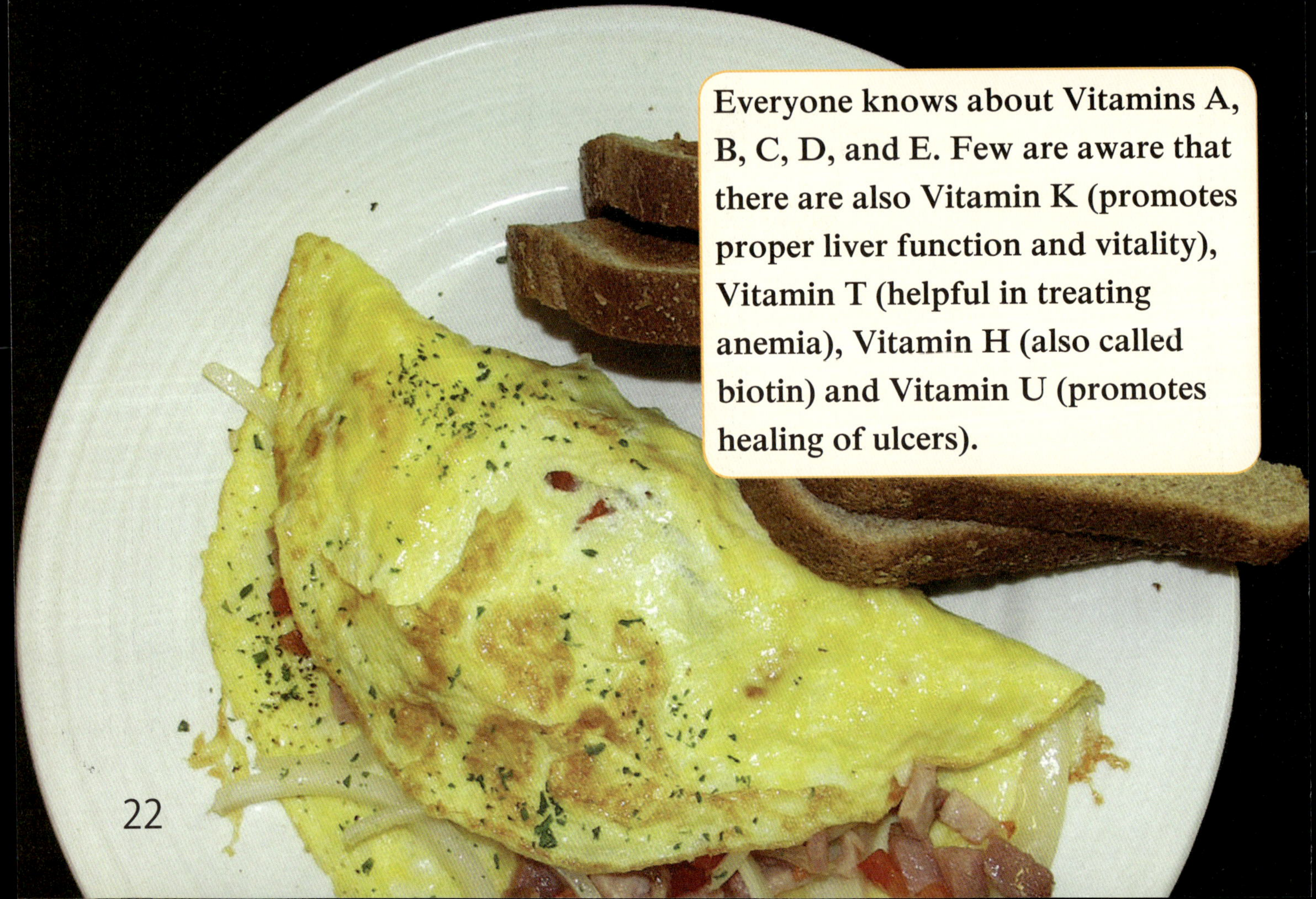

> Everyone knows about Vitamins A, B, C, D, and E. Few are aware that there are also Vitamin K (promotes proper liver function and vitality), Vitamin T (helpful in treating anemia), Vitamin H (also called biotin) and Vitamin U (promotes healing of ulcers).

Some healthy recipes

Chicken soup

Ingredients

- 250 grams breast of chicken
- Cabbage
- 1 carrot
- 3-4 french beans
- 1 capsicum
- 1 onion
- 2-3 cloves of garlic
- Black pepper
- Corn flour
- salt

Method

Chop chicken into small pieces. Mince garlic and chop onion. Grate cabbage. Chop carrot, capsicum and French beans. Grind black pepper.

In a pot, put chicken and water. Add minced garlic, salt and onion. Boil them in a low flame. When the chicken pieces are fully boiled, add all the vegetables and cook again for five minutes.

Take the corn flour and then mix it in cold water. Mix that in the soup and put to boil. The amount of corn flour will decide the consistency of the soup. The thicker you want, the more will be the amount. Serve your soup hot along with bread and butter.

Astonishing fact

In ancient Rome it was considered a sin to eat the flesh of a Woodpecker.

DIET AND RECIPES

Astonishing fact

French fries are actually made in huge factories, frozen, and then processed. The oils and fats are highly processed and highly fatty.

Low-fat grilled chicken salad

Ingredients

- Boneless, skinless chicken breast: 400g
- Potatoes: 300g (cut in half)
- Green beans: 200g
- Orange marmalade: 2 tablespoons
- Leaf lettuce: 3 cups (torn)
- Oranges: 2 (peeled and sectioned)
- Orange juice: 1/4 cup
- Salt and black pepper: Add to taste
- Diced ginger: 1/2 teaspoon

Method

Mix orange juice, marmalade, salt, pepper, orange peel and ginger. Take about 1/4 cup and brush on to the chicken. Then grill until both sides browned. Cut the chicken into slices.

Boil the potatoes for 8 to 10 minutes until tender. Also boil the green beans for 2 to 3 minutes until cooked. Then drain the water.

In a large salad bowl, mix the chicken, orange slices, potatoes and green beans.

Some healthy recipes

Irish chicken stew with dumplings

Ingredients

- 2 cans condensed cream of chicken soup
- 3 cups water
- 1 cup chopped celery
- 2 onions, quartered
- 1 teaspoon salt
- 1/2 teaspoon poultry seasoning
- 1/2 teaspoon ground black pepper
- 4 skinless, boneless chicken breast halves
- 5 carrots, sliced
- 1 package frozen green peas
- 4 potatoes, quartered
- 3 cups baking mix
- 1-1/3 cups milk

> With all the processing that the fast food goes through during manufacturing, a lot of essential nutrients go missing. Fibres, vitamins and minerals get destroyed during this process and what it leaves for you is just unhealthy fats and empty calories.

Method

In a large, heavy pot, combine soup, water, chicken, celery, onion, salt, poultry seasoning and pepper. Cover and cook over low heat for about 1-1/2 hours.

Add potatoes and carrots; cover and cook another 30 minutes.

Remove chicken from pot, shred it and return to the pot. Add peas and cook only 5 minutes longer.

Add dumplings. To make dumplings: Mix baking mix and milk until a soft dough forms. Drop by tablespoonfuls into boiling stew. Cover it for 10 minutes on a low flame, then uncover and simmer for another additional 10 minutes.

DIET AND RECIPES

Spicy baked chicken casserole with peppers, chickpeas and rice

Ingredients

- 1 tbsp Olive oil
- 8 Chicken pieces (thighs and drumsticks)
- 2 Yellow peppers, sliced
- 2 Onions, sliced
- 1 bunch Cilantro
- 3 cloves Garlic
- 1-2 Green chilies
- 1/2 cup canned chickpeas
- 1 cup Basmati rice
- 1 Large lemon
- 3/4 cup Pitted green olives
- 1 1/4 cup Chicken stock

Method

Place a large casserole to heat in the oven. Heat 1 tbsp olive oil in a large frying pan and brown 8 chicken pieces (thighs and drumsticks) all over.

Remove from pan, increase heat and cook 2 sliced yellow peppers and 2 sliced onions until well-browned at the edges.

Add 1 bunch fresh coriander (cilantro), washed and chopped, 3 cloves crushed garlic, 1-2 green chillies, halved, seeded and finely chopped, 3 tsp ground coriander seeds, 100g (1/2 cup) chick peas, 175g (1 cup) basmati rice. Stir well.

Pour in the juice of 1 large lemon and 275ml (1 ¼ cups) chicken stock and bring to boil. Carefully pour this mixture into the pre-heated casserole.

Stir in 100g (3/4 cup) pitted green olives.

Place the chicken pieces on top, cover and bake for 50-60 minutes until the rice is cooked.

Astonishing fact

If you want to lose weight, choose low-fat dairy products – aim for three servings each day such as a glass of skimmed milk, 1 small pot of low-fat yoghurt and a matchbox-sized piece of reduced-fat cheese.

Some healthy recipes

Brownies

Ingredients

- Unsweetened chocolate: 100g
- Flour: 1 cup
- Walnuts: 1/2 cup
- Soy margarine: 1 cup
- Maple sugar: 1 1/2 cup
- Eggs: 4
- Salt: 1/2 teaspoon
- Vanilla extract: 1 tbsp

Method

Pre-heat the oven to 325 degrees.

On low heat, melt and mix chocolate and margarine. Let it cool.

Mix sugar, eggs and vanilla. Whisk until frothy, and add the chocolate mixture.

Add in flour, salt, walnuts and mix well.

Place in a lightly greased pan, and bake for 25 to 30 minutes.

Astonishing fact

Foods that are described as 'low-fat' or 'fat-free' aren't automatically low in calories or calorie-free. In fact, some low-fat products may actually be higher in calories than standard products, thanks to them containing extra sugars and thickeners to boost the flavour and texture.

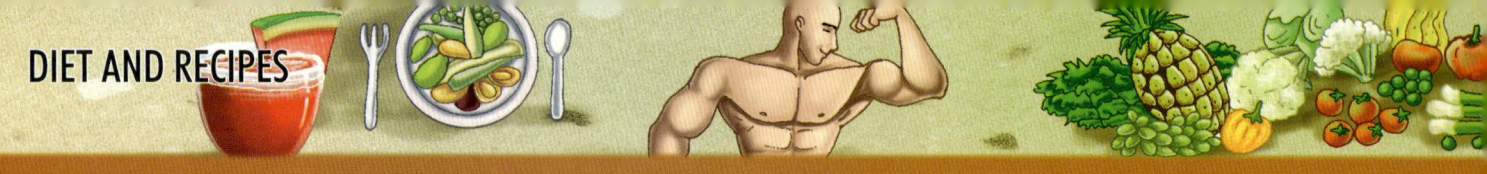

DIET AND RECIPES

Sugar-free muffin

Ingredients

- 1 stick butter
- 3 eggs
- 1 cup pineapple juice
- 1 teaspoon lemon juice
- 2 ½ cups flour
- 1 teaspoon baking soda
- 2 teaspoons baking powder
- ½ teaspoon salt
- 1 cup well-drained crushed pineapple

Method

Preheat oven to 180 degree Celsius.

Combine the butter and eggs in a mixing bowl and beat until the mixture is light and smooth. Add the pineapple juice and lemon juice and mix well. In another smaller bowl, mix together the flour, baking soda, baking powder and salt. Add the flour mixture to the butter and eggs. Mix well. Stir in the crushed pineapple. Do not over mix the batter as it will result in a tough muffin.

Grease a 12-hole muffin tin or line with paper muffin cups. Fill the cups two-thirds full with the muffin mix. Bake for 20 minutes or until a toothpick inserted into the muffins comes out clean.

Astonishing fact

In ancient China and certain parts of India, mouse flesh was considered a great delicacy. In ancient Greece, where the mouse was sacred to Apollo, mice were sometimes devoured by temple priests.

Some healthy recipes

Tuna mixed vegetable pasta

Ingredients

- Tuna can: 200g (drained)
- Mushrooms: 1 1/2 cup (sliced)
- Tomato paste: 1 tablespoon
- Tomato juice: 1 1/4 cup
- Pasta shapes: 350g
- Green onions: 5 (sliced diagonally)
- Grounded peppercorns: 1 teaspoon
- Frozen peas: 1 cup
- Red pepper: 1/2 (seeded and chopped)
- Garlic: 1 clove (crushed)
- Olive oil: 2 tablespoon

Method

Heat the oil in a pan and add mushrooms, garlic and pepper. Cook until mushrooms are soft.

Add in tomato paste, tomato juice and peas. Bring to boil. Then lower the heat and simmer.

Cook the pasta according to package directions. When the pasta is almost done, add the tuna to the sauce and heat gently and add in green onions.

Drain the pasta and serve with the sauce.

Astonishing fact

Half the foods eaten throughout the world today were developed by farmers in the Andes Mountains. Potatoes, maize, sweet potatoes, squash, all varieties of beans, peanuts, manioc, cashews, pineapples, chocolate, avocados, tomatoes, peppers, papayas, strawberries, mulberries and many other foods were first grown in this region.

DIET AND RECIPES

Watermelon juice

Ingredients

- 2 cups chopped seeded watermelon
- 1 cup crushed ice
- 2 teaspoons honey
- 1/4 teaspoon black pepper
- fresh mint

Method

Combine watermelon, ice, honey and black pepper in a blender.

Blend until smooth.

Garnish with mint.

Serve chilled.

Stir well before serving.

Citrus fruit smoothie

Ingredients

- 5 cups grapefruit juice
- 3 cups orange juice
- 1 cup water
- 4 medium firm bananas, cut up and frozen
- 12 frozen unsweetened strawberries

Methods

In a blender, place half of each ingredient; cover and process until smooth.

Pour into a pitcher.

Repeat.

Serve immediately.

Astonishing fact

The staple food of the Kanembu, a tribe living on the shores of Lake Chad in Africa, is Algae. The Kanembu harvest a common variety known as Spirulina from the lake, dry it on the sand, mix it up into a spicy cake, and eat it with tomatoes and chilli peppers.

Test Your MEMORY

1. What is diet?

2. What do you understand by a balanced diet?

3. What are the different types of diet?

4. What is the Body Mass Index?

5. Write about the importance of diet in your life.

6. Write about the role of carbohydrates in your diet.

7. Are fats important in your diet?

8. Write about the role fibres play in your diet.

9. Write about the importance of water in your diet.

10. Write the diet recommended for an ectomorphic body.

11. Write the diet recommended for a mesomorphic body.

12. Write the diet recommended for an endomorphic body.

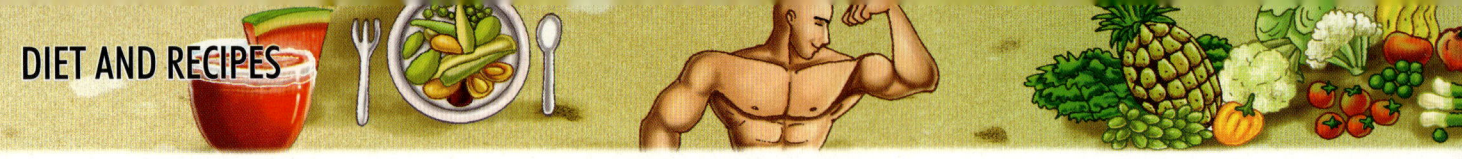

Index

A
Adolphe Quetelet 11

B
balanced diet 3, 4, 5, 13, 14
Body mass index (BMI) 11

C
calories 4, 7, 9, 10, 18, 19, 20, 25, 27
carbohydrates 5, 10, 15, 18, 20

E
ectomorph 18, 19, 20
endomorph 18, 19, 20
exchange-type diet 7

F
fats 5, 15, 16, 18, 24, 25
fibre 5, 10
fixed-menu diet 7
flexible diets 9
formula diets 8

G
glucose 15

L
low-calorie diet 10
low-fat diet 10, 20

M
mesomorph 18, 19, 20
minerals 4, 5, 17, 25

N
nutrients 3, 4, 5, 13, 14, 15, 16, 17, 25

P
pre-packaged meal diet 8
proteins 5, 15, 18

Q
Quetelet Index 11

S
starch 7, 15
sucrose 15

V
vitamins 4, 5, 16, 22, 25

W
water 4, 17, 22, 24, 25, 30

PEGASUS ENCYCLOPEDIA LIBRARY

Food and Nutrition
DISEASES AND ILLNESS

Edited by: Pallabi B. Tomar, Hitesh Iplani
Managing editor: Tapasi De
Designed by: Vijesh Chahal, Anil Kumar, Rohit Kumar
Illustrated by: Suman S. Roy, Tanoy Choudhury
Colouring done by: Vinay Kumar, Kiran Kumari & Pradeep Kumar

CONTENTS

Introduction 3

What is a disease? 4

What is illness? 6

Nutritional deficiency diseases................................... 7

Types of illness 10

Types of nutritional deficiency diseases explained 12

Protein energy malnutrition 27

Prevention and management 29

Test Your Memory... 31

Index.. 32

Introduction

Diseases are one of the factors threatening us from having a properly functional life. Throughout our history, epidemics have caused the extinction of whole populations. Over the last century, man has discovered many micro-organisms that cause diseases in humans and animals, and has learned how to protect himself from them, by either prevention or treatment.

Diseases and illness are any disturbance or irregularity in the normal functioning of the body that probably has a specific cause and identifiable symptoms.

The terms illness and disease are heard on a regular basis. Illness and disease both cause the same feelings of discomfort, pain or unease in people. However, an illness is more of a subjective feeling. This means that there is really no identifiable reason behind the condition. Of course, if the condition behind the illness is identified, it is more often referred to as a disease. However, in more generalized terms, we can define an illness as a state where the person has feelings of pain or discomfort that does not have an identifiable reason.

Astonishing fact

Over 90 per cent of diseases are caused or complicated by stress.

What is a disease?

A disease is any abnormal condition of the body or mind that causes discomfort, dysfunction or distress to the person affected or those in contact with the person. Sometimes the term is used broadly to include injuries, disabilities, syndromes, symptoms, deviant behaviours while in other contexts these maybe considered distinguishable categories.

Pathology is the study of diseases. The subject of systematic classification of diseases is referred to as **Nosology**. The broader body of knowledge about diseases and their treatments is **Medicine**.

The oldest known disease in the world is leprosy.

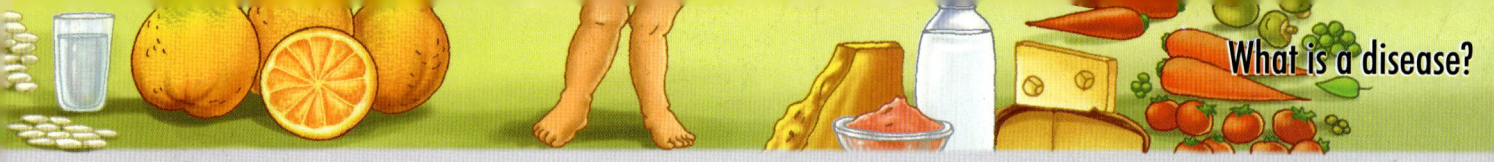

What is a disease?

What we call a disease, is our body's reaction to something that interferes with its normal functioning. An organ remains ill and is eventually destroyed, as long as the source of interference is not removed. A malfunctioning organ can negatively influence other organs and systems (circulatory, nervous, lymphatic) cooperating with it. There is constant struggle between health and illness in the life of our body. We could not stay alive without this struggle.

Disease is the defensive reaction of our body's mechanisms designed to keep us healthy. We all have these mechanisms. They are necessary to remove disorders in the way our body functions. They also give us warning signals when these disorders begin. To stay healthy, we need to listen and understand what our body is trying to communicate to us. Do not treat diseases as your worst enemy. In a sense, they force us to make the first step on the way towards a healthy lifestyle.

Astonishing fact

Each year in America there are about 300,000 deaths that can be attributed to obesity.

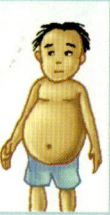

Some diseases, such as influenza are contagious or infectious, and can be transmitted by any of a variety of mechanisms, including droplets from coughs and sneezes, by bites of insects or other vectors, from contaminated water or food, etc.

Other diseases, such as cancer and heart disease are not considered to be due to infection, although micro-organisms may play a role.

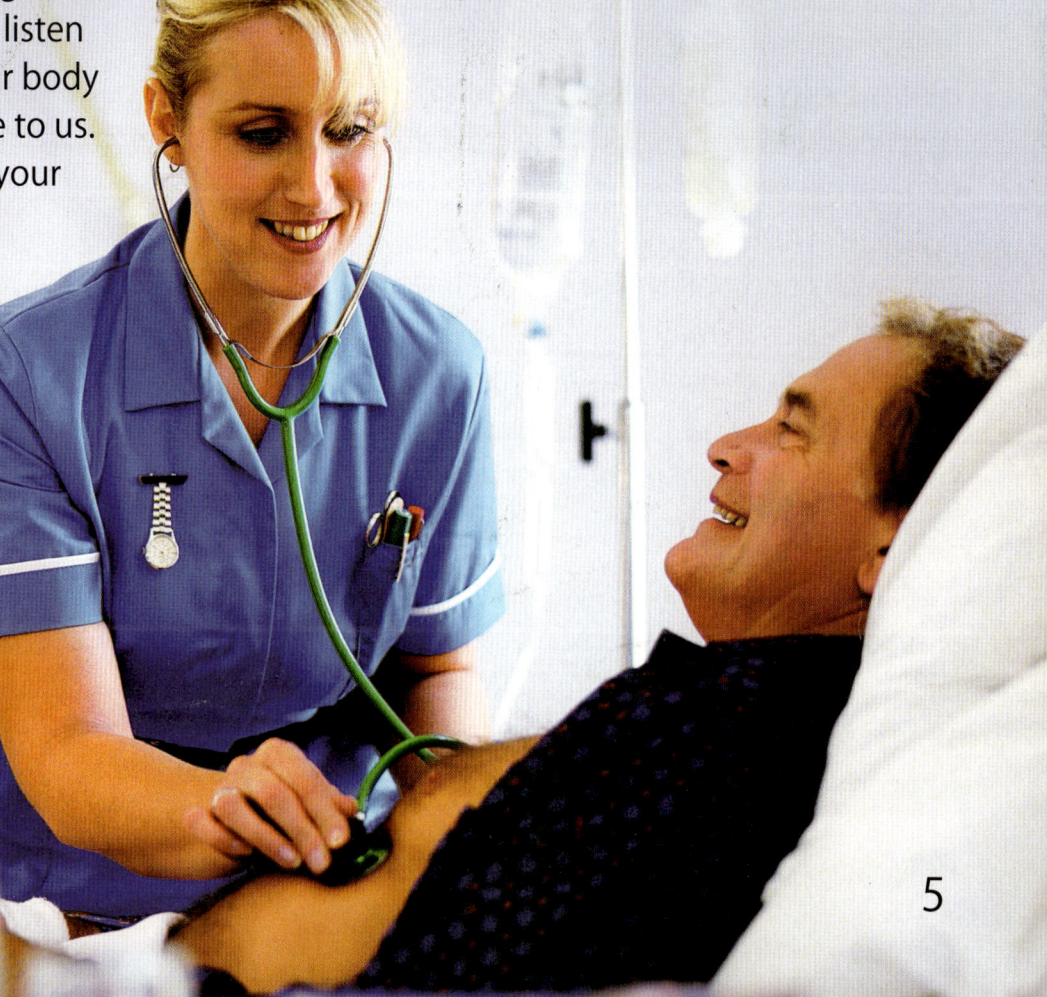

What is illness?

Illness and disease are not necessarily the same. Most people who have a disease will feel they have an illness, while others will feel perfectly healthy. A third group may claim to have an illness although they do not actually have a disease.

> A person afflicted with hexadectylism has six fingers or six toes on one or both hands and feet.

Illness, although often used to mean disease, can also refer to a person's perception of their health, regardless of whether they have a disease or not. A person without any disease may feel unhealthy and believe he has an illness. Another person may feel healthy and believe he does not have an illness even though he may have dangerously high blood pressure which may lead to a fatal heart attack or stroke!

Illness can be a synonymous with disease or it can be a person's perception of having poor health. Disease is an actual physical process which can cause an abnormal condition of the body or mind.

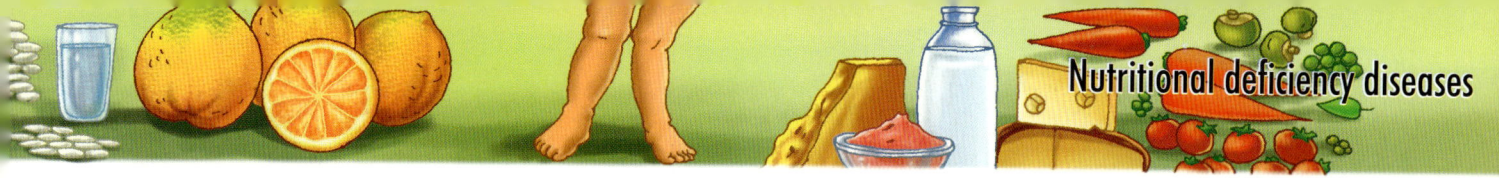

Nutritional deficiency diseases

Nutritional deficiency diseases occur when there is an absence of nutrients which are essential for growth and health. Lack of food leading to either malnutrition or starvation gives rise to these diseases. Another cause for a deficiency disease maybe due to a structural or biological imbalance in the individual's metabolic system.

There are more than 50 known **nutrients** in food. Nutrients enable body tissues to grow and maintain themselves. They contribute to the energy requirements of the individual organism and regulate the processes of the body. Carbohydrates, fats and proteins provide the body with energy. The energy producing component of food is measured in calories. Beside the water and fibre content of foods which are also important for their role in nutrition, the nutrients that serve functions other than energy production can be classified into four different groups— vitamins, fats, proteins and minerals. All are necessary for proper body function and survival.

> It takes about three hours for food to be broken down in the human stomach.

There are about 25 mineral elements in the body usually appearing in the form of simple salts. Those which appear in large amounts are called macro minerals while those that are in small or trace amounts are micro minerals. Some that are essential are calcium, phosphorous, cobalt, copper, fluorine, iodine, iron, sodium, chromium and tin.

DISEASES & ILLNESS

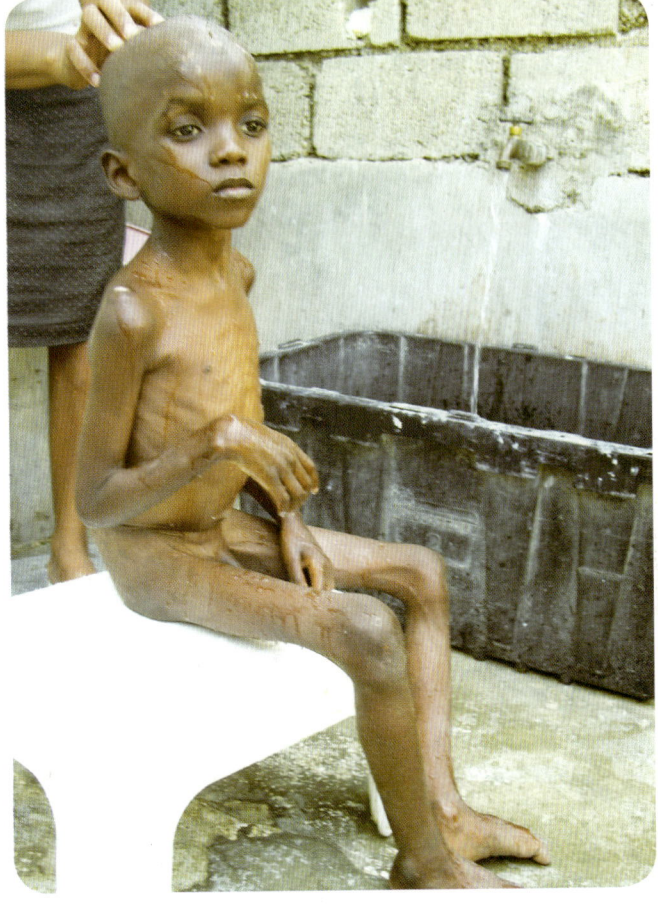

Nutritional deficiencies lead to a variety of health problems, the most prevalent of which are anaemia, beriberi, osteoporosis, pellagra and rickets. Anaemia occurs when the body does not have enough red blood cells to transport oxygen from the lungs to the body's cells. The most common symptom of anaemia is a constant feeling of fatigue. Making sure that one's diet contains the proper amounts of iron, folate and Vitamin B12 can prevent anaemia.

Nutritional deficiencies occur when the body lacks essential nutrients that are obtained from food. In developing countries, such dietary deficiencies are usually the result of poverty and insufficient food supplies. In the developed world, nutritional deficiencies are caused mainly by disorders that limit the body's intake or absorption of nutrients or to unhealthy eating or self-imposed dietary restrictions.

Nutritional deficiencies occur when a person's nutrient intake consistently falls below the recommended requirement. Children between 10–19 years of age face serious nutritional deficiencies worldwide, according to the World Health Organization. About 1,200 million or 19 per cent of adolescents suffer from poor nutrition that hurts their development and growth.

Astonishing fact

Native Americans used to use pumpkin seeds instead of medicine.

Nutritional deficiency diseases

Astonishing fact

It has been medically been proven that laughter is an effective pain killer.

There are two main types of nutritional deficiencies— a general deficiency of calories and nutrients and a deficiency of specific nutrients. A general lack of nutrition maybe caused by poor eating as a result of severe illness or surgery. It may also be due to extreme dieting, general bad eating habits or deliberate starvation. Symptoms of a general deficiency may include weight loss, muscle weakness, tiredness, as well as skin and hair disorders.

Specific nutritional deficiencies may occur if people limit their diets because of certain beliefs. Specific nutritional deficiencies may result in a variety of disorders. These include iron deficiency like anaemia and the bone disorders like osteomalacia and rickets caused by a lack of calcium or Vitamin D. Vegetarians who fail to eat a balanced diet may often suffer from a lack of iron and other micronutrients. Vegetarians will suffer from a deficiency of Vitamin B12 if they do not eat B12 fortified foods.

Nutritional deficiency is a state where there are insufficient nutrients present for the body to function normally. Nutritional deficiency can affect one or more bodily functions and vary greatly in severity. Being deficient in a particular nutrient can cause the body to behave in a number of abnormal ways. For example, deficiency in calcium and phosphorus may cause problems for bone structure, nails and hair, whereas being deficient in protein will affect muscle and energy levels.

Types of illness

Physical

Conditions of the body or mind that cause pain, dysfunction or distress to the person affected or those in contact with the person can be deemed an illness. Sometimes the term is used broadly to include injuries, disabilities, syndromes, infections, symptoms, deviant behaviours. A pathogen or infectious agent is a biological agent that causes disease or illness to its host. A passenger virus is a virus that simply hitchhikes in the body of a person or infects the body without causing symptoms, illness or disease. Food borne illness or food poisoning is any illness resulting from the consumption of food contaminated with pathogenic bacteria, toxins, viruses or parasites.

3000 children die every day in Africa because of malaria.

Types of illness

Mental

Mental illnesses are medical conditions that disrupt a person's thinking, feeling, mood, ability to relate to others and daily functioning. Just as diabetes is a disorder of the pancreas, mental illnesses are medical conditions that often result in a lessened capacity for coping with the ordinary demands of life.

Serious mental illnesses include major depression, schizophrenia, bipolar disorder, obsessive compulsive disorder (OCD), panic disorder, post traumatic stress disorder (PTSD) and borderline personality disorder. The good news about mental illness is that recovery is possible.

Mental illnesses can affect persons of any age, race, religion or income. Mental illnesses are not the result of personal weakness, lack of character or poor upbringing. Mental illnesses are treatable. Most people diagnosed with a serious mental illness can experience relief from their symptoms by actively participating in an individual treatment plan.

> **Vitamin A was given the first letter of the alphabet, as it was the first to be discovered.**

Types of nutritional deficiency diseases explained

Vitamin A

Functions

Vitamin A is a fat-soluble organic compound that the body needs to remain healthy. Humans cannot make Vitamin A, so they must get it from foods in their diet. Vitamin A is sometimes called **retinol**.

Vitamin A affects many different systems of the body. It is especially important to maintaining good vision, a healthy immune system and strong bones. Vitamin A also helps turn on and off certain genes (gene expression) during cell division and differentiation. Getting the correct amount—not too little and not too much—of Vitamin A is essential for health. People who get too little Vitamin A have vision defects, are more likely to have damaged cells in the lining of body cavities and are more susceptible to infection. People who get too much Vitamin A have weakened bones that tend to break easily and have a chronic feeling of illness that includes headache, nausea, irritability, fatigue and muscle and joint pain. Excess Vitamin A can also cause birth defects in a developing foetus.

> The purpose of tonsils is to destroy foreign substances that are swallowed or breathed in.

Types of nutritional deficiency diseases explained

Food sources

Vitamin A occurs in nature in two forms— preformed Vitamin A and proVitamin A, or carotene. Sources of Vitamin A can be divided into two groups— one is animal source and the other is vegetable source. Vitamin A comes from animal sources such as eggs and meat. Vitamin A in the form of retinyl palmitate, is found in beef, calf, chicken liver, eggs and fish liver oils as well as dairy products including whole milk, whole milk yogurt, whole milk cottage cheese, butter and cheese. The vegetable sources of beta-carotene are fat and cholesterol free. The body regulates the conversion of beta-carotene to Vitamin A, based on the body's needs. Sources of beta-carotene are carrots, pumpkin, sweet potatoes, winter squashes, cantaloupe, pink grapefruit, apricots, broccoli, spinach and most dark green, leafy vegetables.

Diseases

- A deficiency of Vitamin A may lead to eye problems with dryness of the conjunctiva and cornea, dry skin and hair, night blindness as well as poor growth.

- The eyes are obvious indicators of Vitamin A deficiency. One of the first symptoms is night blindness.

- Other indicators of Vitamin A deficiency include susceptibility to colds, flu, bacterial and viral infections, especially of the respiratory and urinary tract.

Astonishing fact

Teenagers are 50 per cent more vulnerable to colds than people over fifty.

DISEASES & ILLNESS

Astonishing fact

Diabetes was the third leading cause of death by disease in America. It has increased by 50 per cent since 1965, and today affects at least 15 million people.

Vitamin D

Functions

It is a fat soluble vitamin that is found in food and can also be made in your body after exposure to ultraviolet rays from the sun. Vitamin D performs many vital functions in the body. It is required for the development of strong teeth and bones and maintains their structure. Vitamin D is essential for the healthy functioning of the parathyroid gland which regulates the levels of calcium in the body. Secondly, it maintains the balance between the calcium in the blood and the calcium in the bones. Next, Vitamin D helps in the absorption of calcium, phosphate and other minerals. Finally, it regulates the excretion of calcium and phosphate by the kidneys.

Vitamin D has many therapeutic uses. Since it increases the absorption of calcium and regulates the deposition of minerals in the teeth and bones, it is used to treat arthritis and repair bones. Moreover, it is beneficial in cases of lowered immunity, chronic fatigue and even depression. It has been found that Vitamin D made in the presence of sunlight slows down the growth of cancer, and prevents degenerative diseases like heart diseases, blood pressure and muscular weakness.

Types of nutritional deficiency diseases explained

Food sources

As we know, the main source of Vitamin D comes from exposure to the sun's UVB rays but besides this, it is can also be found in various food items like fish (herring, mackerel, salmon, and sardines), egg yolks, orange juice, breakfast cereals, green leafy vegetables, fish liver oils, yogurt, cheese, etc. Fortified foods are other common sources of Vitamin D. In fact, one cup of Vitamin D fortified milk provides one-half of the recommended daily intakes for people between the ages of 19 and 50.

Nowadays, there are many multivitamins, calcium and Vitamin D supplements available to maintain Vitamin D concentration in the body and to overcome its deficiency. However, before taking any Vitamin D supplement, do consult your doctor as just like Vitamin D deficiency can lead to various health problems; its excess can also cause adverse effects on the body.

Diseases

Deficiency of Vitamin D has serious consequences, including retarded growth, defective teeth and dental caries. Moreover, its deficiency prevents assimilation of other minerals, and causes lowered immunity and premature aging. Since a shortage of Vitamin D leads to a reduction of calcium and phosphate, the bone formation is affected, leading to rickets in children and osteoporosis and conditions related to weak bones in adults. Other symptoms include muscular weakness, cramps, reduced energy and even convulsions.

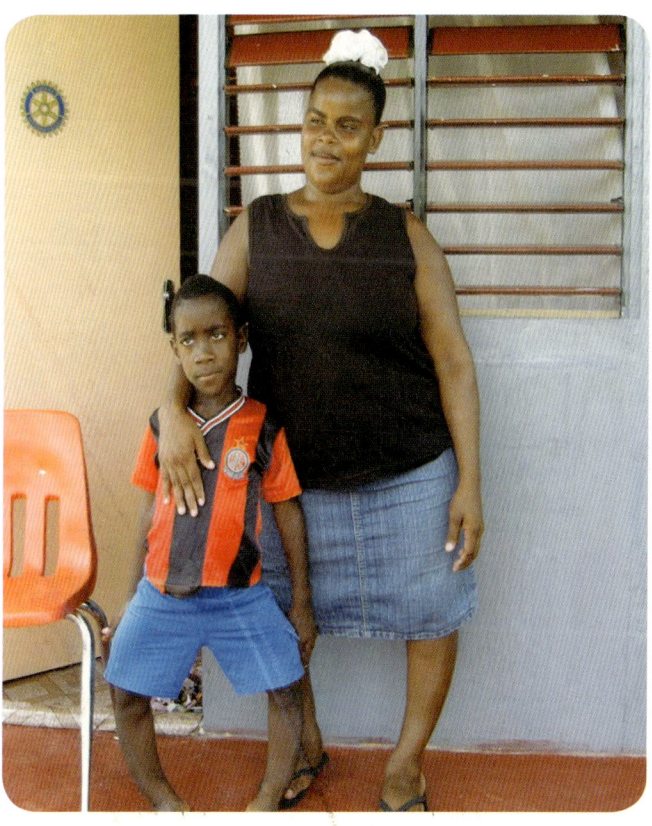

Astonishing fact

In 1918 and 1919 a world epidemic of simple Influenza killed 20 million people in the United States and Europe.

15

Vitamin B complex

Functions

The Vitamin B complex consists of eight water soluble vitamins. It is present in the form of Vitamins B1, B2, B3, B5, B6, B12, folic acid and biotin. The B vitamins work together to boost metabolism, enhance the immune system and nervous system, keep the skin and muscles healthy, encourage cell growth and division and other benefits to your body. The main functions of this vitamin includes:

1. **B1/Thiamine**

   Breaks down carbohydrates to release energy; helps in normal functioning of the nervous system; helps to maintain the acidity level in the stomach and keeps the appetite normal.

2. **B3/Niacin**

   Helps to release energy from food, keeps the skin, mouth and digestive tract healthy. It is also vital for healthy mental functioning, helps to promote blood circulation and maintains the blood pressure.

3. **B2/Riboflavin**

   This helps to convert proteins, fats and carbohydrates into energy and is integral in maintaining healthy skin and eyes.

4. **B5/ Pantothenic acid**

   This helps in releasing energy from food, maintains normal functioning of the adrenal gland and aids formations of antibodies.

5. **B6/ Pyridoxine**

   This is required for protein metabolism, fluid balance and healthy maintenance of red blood cells.

6. **B12**

   This vitamin helps in red blood cell production and maintenance of healthy red blood cells. Deficiency of this vitamin can make people mentally lethargic, can cause shivering in the body and causes anaemia.

7. **Folic acid**

   Essential for growth and reproduction of red blood cells

8. **Biotin**

   Keeps the skin and hair healthy

Astonishing fact

One cannot catch cold at the North Pole in winter; neither can one contract the flu, nor most of the ailments transmitted viruses and germs. The winter temperature is so low in this part of the world that none of the standard disease causing micro-organisms can survive.

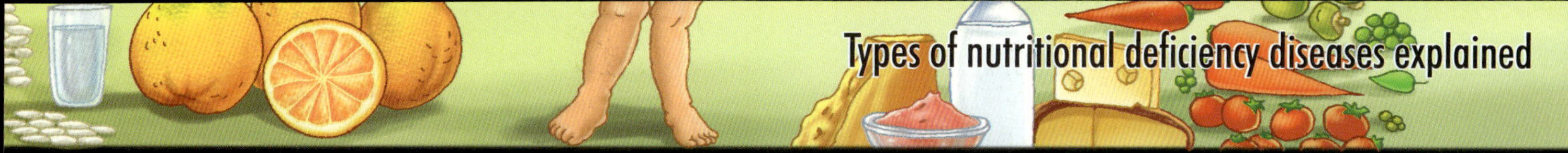

Food sources

- B1 and B2 are found in cereals and whole grains. B1 is also found in potatoes, pork, seafood, liver and kidney beans. B2 is found in enriched bread, dairy products, liver and green leafy vegetables.

- B3 is found in liver, fish, chicken, lean red meat, nuts, whole grains and dried beans.

- B5 is found in almost all foods.

- B6 is found in fish, liver, pork, chicken, potatoes, wheat germ, bananas and dried beans.

- B7 is made by intestinal bacteria and is also in peanuts, liver, egg yolks, bananas, mushrooms, watermelon and grapefruit.

- B9 is in green leafy vegetables, liver, citrus fruits, mushrooms, nuts, peas, dried beans and wheat bread.

- B12 is found in eggs, meat, poultry, shellfish, milk and milk products.

Diseases

Several deficiency diseases may result from the lack of B-vitamins. These include:

Vitamin	Disease
Vitamin B1	Deficiency causes beriberi, weight loss, emotional disturbances, swelling of bodily tissues, amnesia.
Vitamin B2 (Riboflavin)	Deficiency causes cracks in the lips, high sensitivity to sunlight, inflammation of the tongue, syphilis.
Vitamin B3 (Niacin)	Deficiency causes pellagra, mental confusion and even death.
Vitamin B6	Deficiency may lead to anaemia, dermatitis, high blood pressure.
Vitamin B7	Deficiency may lead to impaired growth and neurological disorders in infants.
Folic acid	Deficiency in pregnant women can lead to birth defects.
Vitamin B12	Deficiency causes pernicious anaemia, memory loss and other cognitive diseases.

Astonishing fact

A popular superstition is that if you put a piece of bread in a baby's crib, it will keep away diseases!

Vitamin C

Functions

Vitamin C is a water-soluble, antioxidant vitamin, also known as ascorbic acid. Vitamin C helps in the absorption of iron and maintains capillaries, bones and teeth. Humans do not have the ability to make their own Vitamin C. Therefore, we must obtain Vitamin C through our diet.

Vitamin C benefits us a lot. The best benefit offered by Vitamin C is collagen formation. Collagen is essentially a protein substance that helps keeping all the cells together. Vitamin C aids in the formation of collagen. Without Vitamin C, the formation of collagen is interrupted. Vitamin C is present and active within the cell wall where it aids in modifying pro-collagen into collagen.

Vitamin C helps in the absorption of iron as previously mentioned. Iron is essential to keep us healthy and vibrant. It maintains a healthy and clear skin, fresh complexion and healthy gums and teeth. It offers a healthy functioning for all glands and organs including adrenal and thyroid glands. It also aids in relieving all sort of stressors, both physical and psychological.

Asthma affects one in fifteen children under the age of eighteen.

DISEASES & ILLNESS

Food sources

Vitamin C is obtained from fruits and vegetables. Some excellent sources of Vitamin C are oranges, green peppers, watermelon, papaya, grapefruit, cantaloupe, strawberries, kiwi, mango, broccoli, tomatoes, Brussels sprouts, cauliflower, cabbage and citrus juices or juices fortified with Vitamin C.

Vitamin C is sensitive to light, air, and heat, so it is best to eat fruits and vegetables raw or minimally cooked in order to retain their full Vitamin C content.

Diseases

Scurvy is the main disease that is caused by the deficiency of Vitamin C, which is characterized by easily bruised skin, muscle fatigue, soft swollen gums, decreased wound healing and haemorrhaging, osteoporosis and anaemia. The primary cause of Vitamin C deficiency is poor diet. Vitamin C deficiency may develop in people who eat only such foods as dried meat, tea, toast and canned vegetables. Pregnancy, breastfeeding, surgery, and burns can significantly increase the body's requirements for Vitamin C and the risk of Vitamin C deficiency.

The symptoms of the deficiency of Vitamin C may include irritability, depression, weight loss, fatigue and general weakness. The gums become swollen, purple and spongy. The teeth eventually loosen. Infections may develop and wounds do not heal.

Calcium

Functions

Calcium plays an important role in the maintenance of health. It has been called the prime instigator of vital activity.

- This mineral is essential for the proper development of bones and teeth.

- It is necessary for the normal action of the heart and all muscle activity.

- It aids the clotting process of the blood and stimulates enzymes in the digestive process.

- Calcium is required for proper foetal growth, for normal health of the mother during pregnancy and lactation and for the secretion of breast milk.

- It speeds all the healing processes and controls the conduction mechanism in the nerve tissues so that messages travel fast enough for the functioning of the body.

- It is essential for proper utilization of phosphorus and Vitamin D, Vitamin A and Vitamin C.

Milk

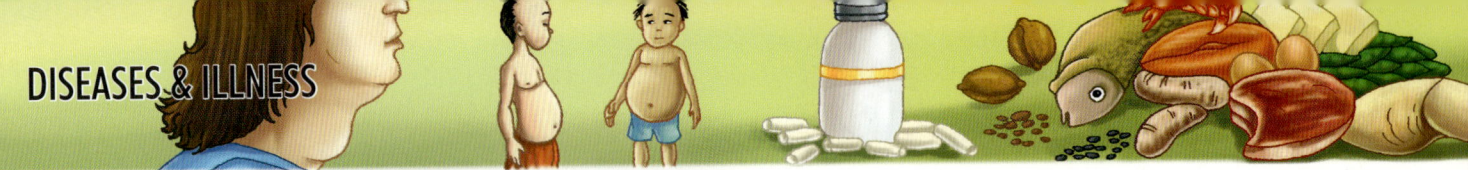

DISEASES & ILLNESS

Food sources

Milk and milk products such as non-fat cheese, cottage cheese and yogurt are sources of calcium. Other sources of calcium include dark green leafy vegetables, spinach, kale, turnip greens, cabbage, collard, mustard, seaweeds, alfalfa, broccoli, canned fish (especially sardines, clams, oysters and salmon) with bones and cooked dried beans and peas.

Diseases

Some of the indications of calcium deficiencies include skeletal abnormalities, such as osteopenia, osteomalacia, osteoporosis and rickets.

> Red blood cells are created inside the marrow of your bones. They serve the important role of carrying blood around your body.

Osteomalacia is a failure to mineralize the bone matrix, resulting in a reduction of the mineral content of the bone. In children, osteomalacia is known as rickets. When children have rickets, their bones become soft and flexible, bending in ways normal bones would not.

Osteopenia is the presence of less than normal amount of bone. Osteopenia, if not treated, may result in osteoporosis.

Osteoporosis occurs when the composition of the bone is normal, but the mass is so reduced that the skeleton loses its strength and becomes unable to perform its supporting role in the body. In this case, fractures may occur due to minor falls and bumps, or bones may even break under their own weight. People with osteoporosis may have a hump in their backs, scoliosis (curvature of the spine), kyphosis (rounded shoulders) or lose height. These conditions maybe caused by the buckling of their weakened spines, no longer being strong enough to hold the body upright.

The bones act as a reservoir for calcium. When the amount of calcium in the blood supply dips too low, calcium is borrowed from the bones. It is returned to the bones from calcium supplied through the diet. When diets are low in the mineral, there may not be sufficient amounts available to be returned to the bones. Over time, this net loss can lead to osteopenia or osteoporosis.

Types of nutritional deficiency diseases explained

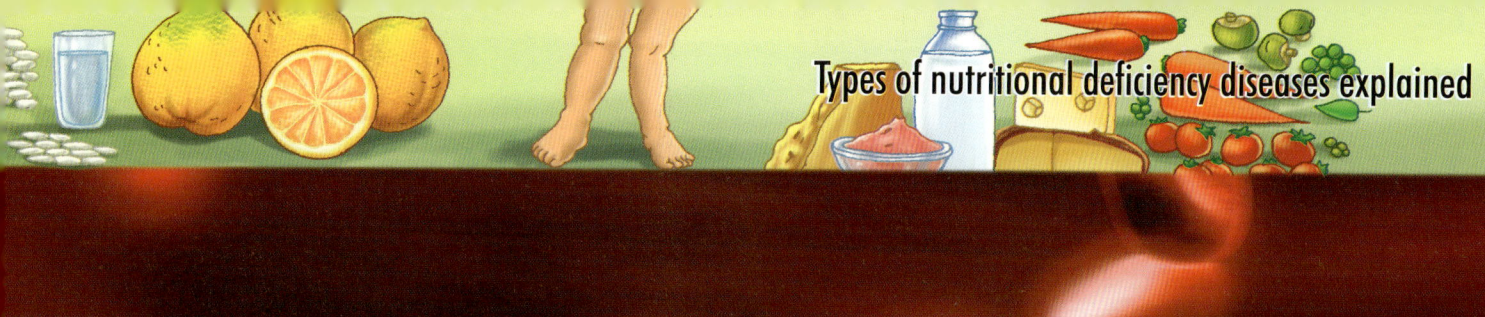

Iron

Functions

Iron is vital to the health of the human body and is found in every human cell, primarily linked with protein to form the oxygen-carrying molecule haemoglobin. The human body contains approximately 4 grams of iron.

Iron serves as the core of the haemoglobin molecule, which is the oxygen-carrying component of the red blood cell. Red blood cells pick up oxygen from the lungs and distribute the oxygen to the tissues throughout the body. The ability of red blood cells to carry oxygen is attributed to the presence of iron in the haemoglobin molecule.

If we lack iron, we will produce less haemoglobin, and therefore supply less oxygen to our tissues. Iron is also an important constituent of another protein called **myoglobin**. Myoglobin, like haemoglobin, is an oxygen-carrying molecule, which distributes oxygen to muscles cells, especially to skeletal muscles and to the heart.

Astonishing fact

Around 7 million people die every year from food poisoning out of a total of around 70 million cases. Careful food preparation and storage is vital in order to avoid dangerous toxins, viruses and bacteria.

DISEASES & ILLNESS

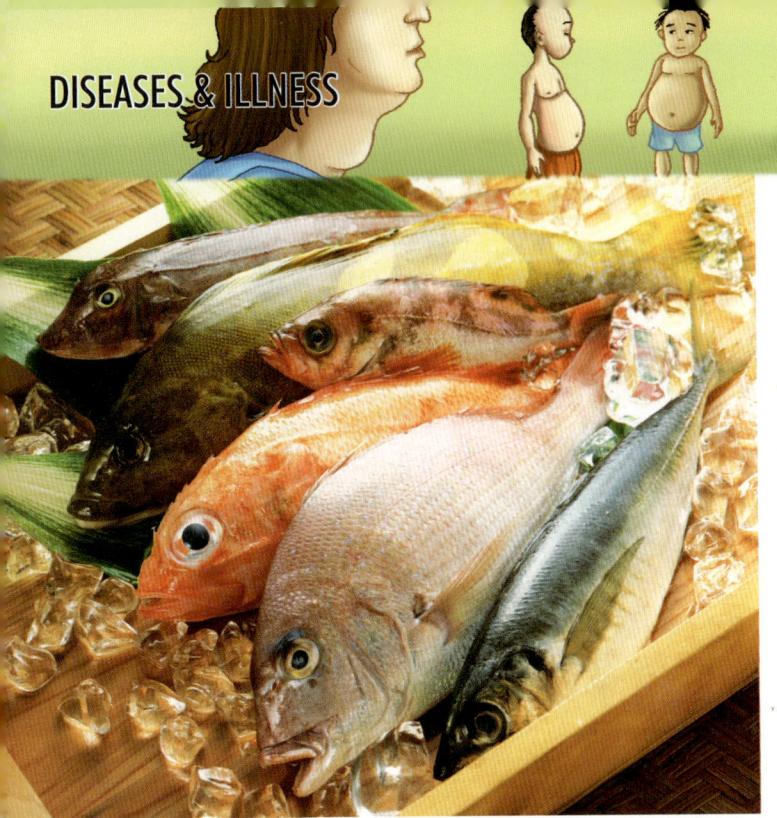

Food sources

The body does not produce iron, so it is important to get it from the diet. Poultry, lean meats, eggs, fish, beans and nuts are good sources of iron. It is also found in whole grain cereals, legumes, pulses, lentils, jaggery and fish. Vegetable sources include green leafy ones like turnip greens and cauliflower, while fruits include raisins, watermelons, currants and dried dates. Some iron is also absorbed by food cooked in iron vessels.

Iron is an essential trace element required for healthy blood, growth and vitality. Lack of iron or its absorption has serious consequences, so one must take iron rich food and keep the gastro-intestinal tract healthy to aid its absorption. Good sources are iron-rich fruits, which have their own acids and enzymes required for the digestion and assimilation of iron.

Diseases

Iron deficiency causes microcytic and hypochromic anaemia, a condition characterized by underdeveloped red blood cells that lack haemoglobin, thereby reducing the oxygen carrying capacity of red blood cells. But even before iron deficiency anaemia develops, people with poor iron status may experience a variety of symptoms including fatigue, weakness, loss of stamina, decreased ability to concentrate, increased susceptibility to infections, hair loss, dizziness, headaches, brittle nails, lethargy and depression.

Obesity can increase the chances of developing diseases such as type 2 diabetes and heart disease.

Types of nutritional deficiency diseases explained

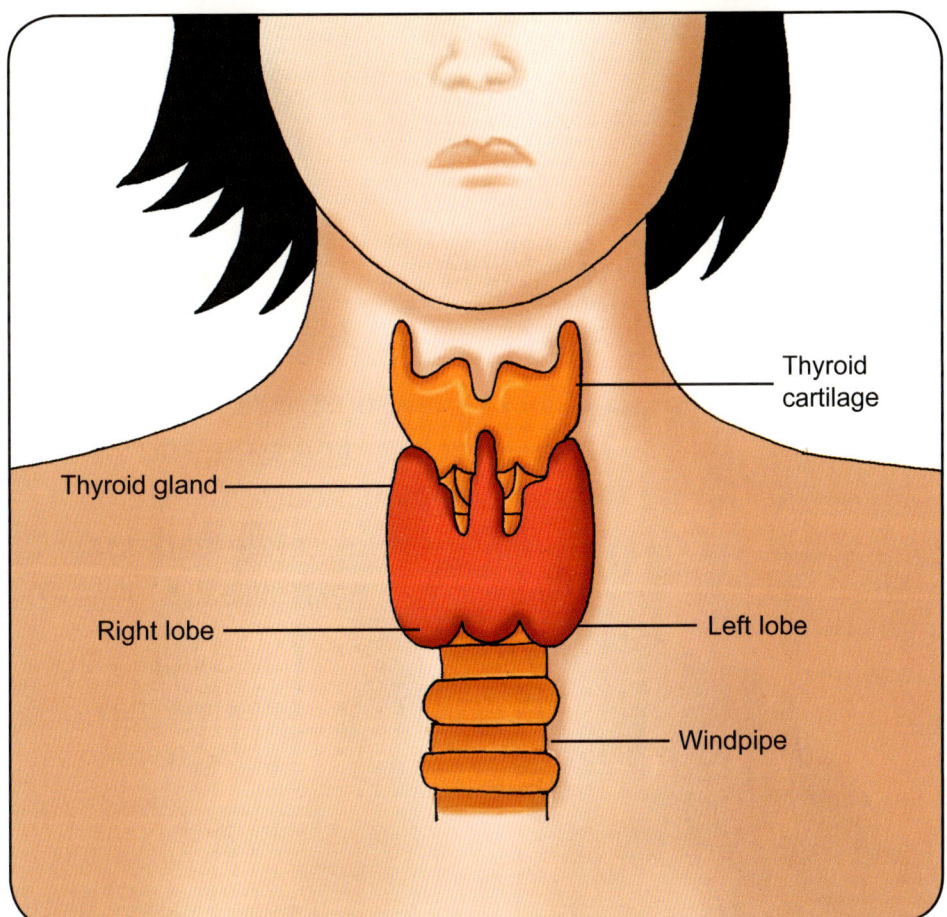

Iodine

Functions

Iodine is an essential mineral for the survival and sustenance of the human body, and a lack of iodine in the diet can lead to many iodine deficiency disorders (IDD). These are conditions that arise due to a lack of necessary iodine levels in the body and they can be cured by including healthy levels of iodine in one's diet.

The thyroid gland needs iodine to produce the body hormone thyroxine, which regulates the release of energy in the body. Iodine is mainly found in the thyroid glands and is an indispensable element for the body metabolism. Without it, a person gains weight and is fatigued. On the other hand, with hyperthyroid, a person loses weight and is hyperactive.

- Iodine prevents the development of simple goitre.
- Iodine plays a role in the development of hair, fingernails, skin and teeth.

In 2007, around 13 per cent of all deaths worldwide was caused by cancer. The branch of medicine related to cancer study and treatment is known as oncology.

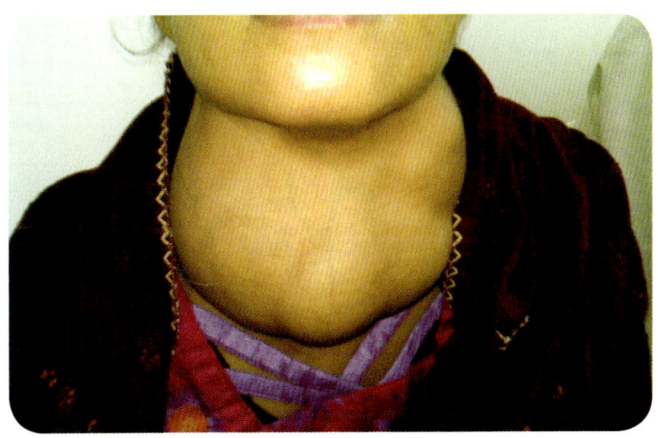

25

DISEASES & ILLNESS

- Its deficiency may also causes deafness and poor learning.
- Iodine deficiency or total loss will affect our mental and physical activity, obesity and hardening of blood vessels.
- A dietary lack of iodine may cause anaemia, tiredness, laziness, a slow pulse, low blood pressure and high blood cholesterol/ triglyceride leading to heart disease.
- In children lack of iodine may lead to mental retardation, enlarged thyroid gland, defective speech and clumsy gait.

Food sources

Iodine is available in traces in water, food and common salts. Sea weeds and spongy shells are very rich in iodine. The best sources are sea fish, sea salt, green vegetables and leaves like spinach grown on iodine rich soil. The common sources are milk, meat and cereals. About 90 per cent of the iodine intake is obtained from the food consumed and the remainder from the water.

Diseases

- Iodine deficiency leads to enlargement of thyroid gland known as simple **goitre** which involves swelling of feet or toes, enlarged glands, excessive hunger, neuralgic pains in the heart, etc.

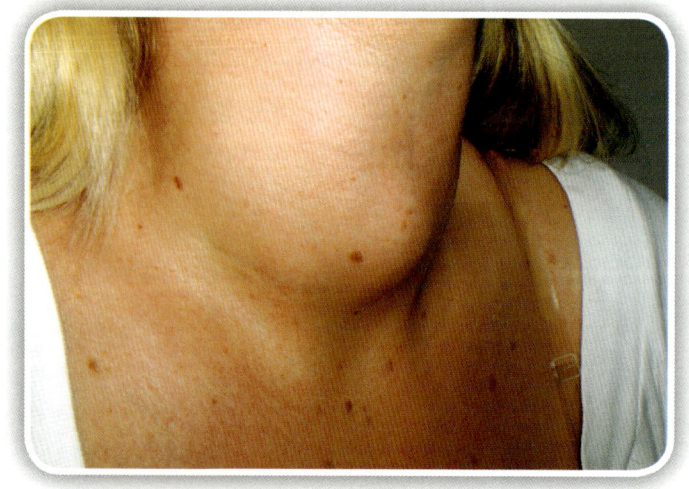

Protein energy malnutrition

Protein-energy malnutrition (PEM) is a potentially fatal body-depletion disorder. It is the leading cause of death in children in developing countries.

PEM is also referred to as protein-calorie malnutrition. It develops in children whose consumption of protein and energy (measured by calories) is insufficient to satisfy their nutritional needs. While pure protein deficiency can occur when a person's diet provides enough energy but lacks an adequate amount of protein, in most cases deficiency will exist in both total calorie and protein intake. PEM may also occur in children with illnesses that leave them unable to absorb vital nutrients or convert them to the energy essential for healthy tissue formation and organ function.

Primary PEM results from a diet that lacks sufficient sources of protein. Secondary PEM is more common in the United States, where it usually occurs as a complication of AIDS, cancer, chronic kidney failure, inflammatory bowel disease and other illnesses that impair the body's ability to absorb or use nutrients or to compensate for nutrient losses. PEM can develop gradually in a child who has a chronic illness or experiences chronic semi-starvation. It may appear suddenly in a patient who has an acute illness.

Kwashiorkor, also called wet protein-energy malnutrition, is a form of PEM characterized primarily by protein deficiency. This condition usually appears at about the age of 12 months when breast-feeding is discontinued, but it can develop at any time during a child's formative years. It causes fluid retention (edema); dry, peeling skin and hair discoloration.

Marasmus, a PEM disorder, is caused by total calorie/energy depletion rather than primarily protein calorie/energy depletion. Marasmus is characterized by stunted growth and wasting of muscle and tissue. Marasmus usually develops between the ages of six months and one year in children who have been weaned from breast milk or who suffer from weakening conditions such as chronic diarrhoea.

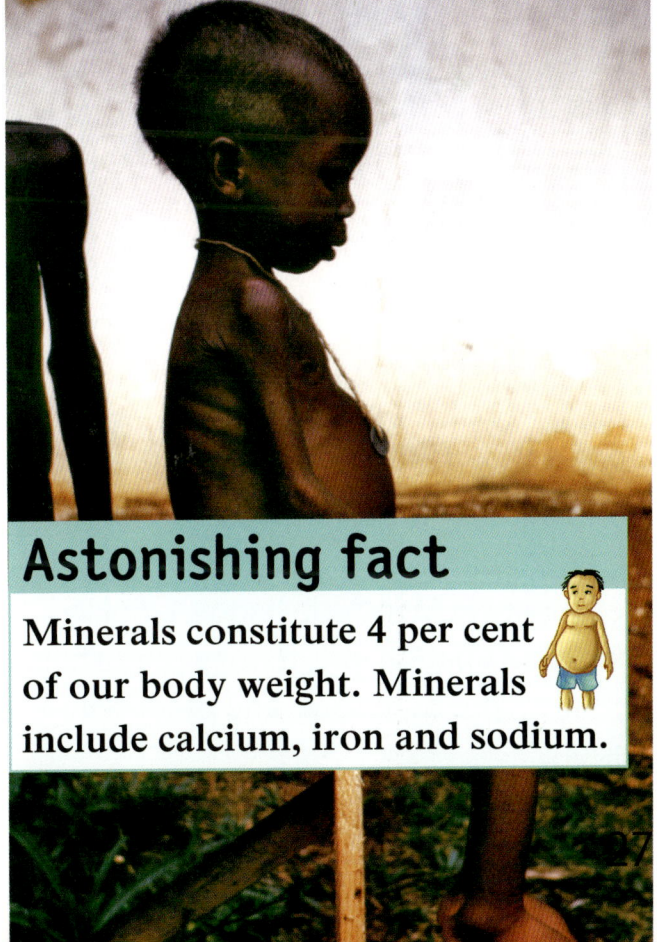

Astonishing fact

Minerals constitute 4 per cent of our body weight. Minerals include calcium, iron and sodium.

DISEASES & ILLNESS

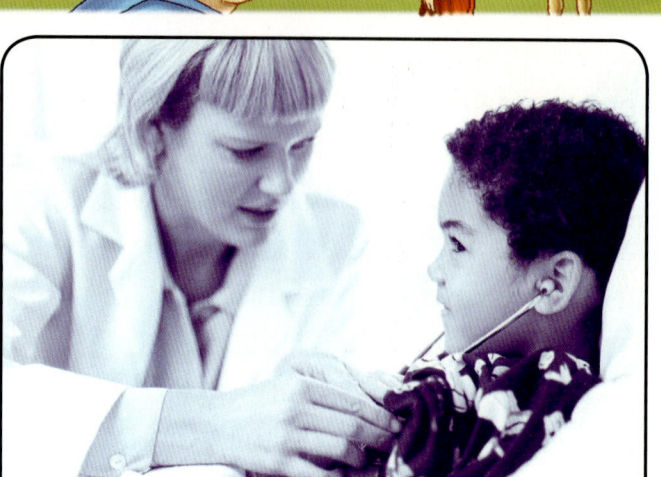

Secondary PEM symptoms range from mild to severe, and can alter the form or function of almost every organ in the body. The type and intensity of symptoms depend on the patient's prior nutritional status, the nature of the underlying disease, and the speed at which the PEM is progressing.

Mild, moderate and severe classifications for PEM have not been precisely defined, but patients who lose 10–20 per cent of their body weight without trying may have moderate PEM. This level of PEM is characterized by a weakened grip and inability to perform high-energy tasks.

Losing 20 per cent of body weight or more is generally classified as severe PEM. Children with this condition cannot eat normal-sized meals. They have slow heart rates and low blood pressure and body temperatures. Other symptoms of severe secondary PEM include baggy, wrinkled skin, constipation, dry, thin, or brittle hair, lethargy, pressure sores and other skin lesions.

Children suffering from kwashiorkor often have extremely thin arms and legs, but liver enlargement and ascites (abnormal accumulation of fluid) can distend the abdomen and disguise weight loss. Hair may turn red or yellow. Anaemia, diarrhoea, fluid and electrolyte disorders are common. The body's immune system is often weakened, behavioural development is slow and mental retardation may occur. Children may grow to normal height but are abnormally thin.

Profound weakness accompanies severe marasmus. Since the body breaks down its own tissue to use for energy, children with this condition lose all their body fat and muscle strength, and acquire a skeletal appearance most noticeable in the hands and in the temporal muscle in front of and above each ear. Children with marasmus are small for their age. Since their immune systems are weakened, they suffer from frequent infections. Other symptoms include loss of appetite, diarrhoea, skin that is dry and baggy, sparse hair that is dull brown or reddish yellow, mental retardation, behavioural retardation, low body temperature (hypothermia) and slow pulse and breathing rates.

Astonishing fact

Eggs contain the highest quality food protein known. All parts of an egg are edible, including the shell which has high calcium content.

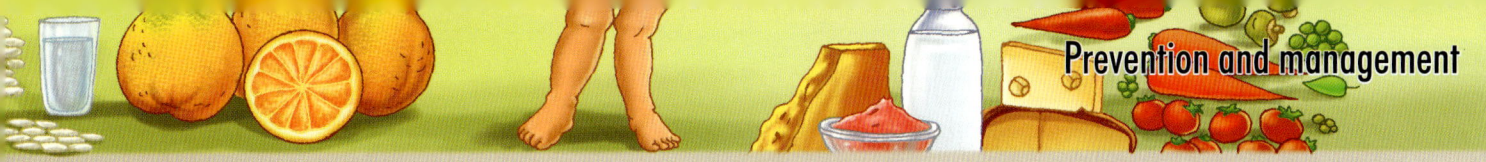

Prevention and management

Prevention and management

Nutritional deficiency diseases result primarily from a diet that does not have enough of the nutrients that are essential to health or development. Another cause is that an individual may not be able to utilize properly the nutrients consumed in the diet. Deficiency diseases may result from a person's abnormally high metabolic needs for a nutrient or from some imbalance in the nutrients ingested. Certain drugs or medicines may also affect nutrient use. Deficiency diseases often result from insufficient food intake or a poorly balanced diet, but may also be caused by ill health (diarrhoea, parasitic infections, cancer, AIDS). The most severe deficiency disease is starvation, where there is marked weight reduction, loss of fat and other tissues, including from the liver and intestines. Most systems are affected, including the body's immune system. The skin and hair become dry. Diarrhoea often develops, and the sufferer may die of secondary infection. Nutritional deficiency contributes to much of the ill health in developing countries. The most important forms of malnutrition are protein-energy malnutrition, iodine deficiency disorders, vitamin A deficiency and nutritional anaemia.

Nutrients are the cornerstone of a healthy diet. If your diet doesn't include the proper nutrients, your health suffers. If you don't eat and drink nutritious food and beverages

- Your bones may bend or break (not enough calcium).
- Your gums may bleed (not enough Vitamin C).
- Your blood may not carry oxygen to every cell (not enough iron).

Astonishing fact

Food allergies are fairly common amongst adults and even more so among children. Around 2 per cent of adults and 8 per cent of children suffer from some type of food allergy where the immune system makes a mistake and thinks a certain food protein is dangerous and attacks it.

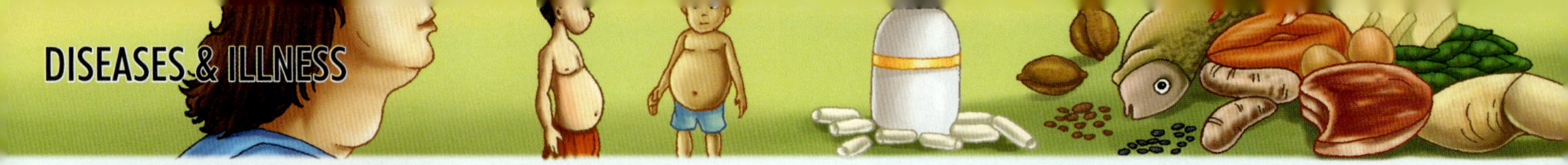

DISEASES & ILLNESS

Nutrition from the food you eat provides the energy and building materials you need to construct and maintain every organ and system. Virtually all food gives you energy, even when it does not give you nutrients. The amount of energy in food is measured in calories, the amount of heat produced when food is burned in your body cells. Food is the fuel on which your body runs. Without enough food, you don't have enough energy.

The body requires carbohydrates, fats, proteins, vitamins and minerals to maintain healthy organs, bones, muscles, nerves and to produce hormones and chemicals that are necessary for the proper function of organs. Vitamins and minerals are naturally occurring substances that are essential for the growth and function of the body. Vitamins and minerals are both necessary for normal chemical reactions (metabolism) in the body.

Vitamins and mineral supplements are important both in preventing deficiency states as well as in preventing diseases. Most diseases resulting from Vitamin deficiencies such as scurvy (Vitamin C deficiency), blindness (Vitamin A deficiency), and beriberi (thiamine deficiency) occur mainly in third-world countries.

Astonishing fact

Lack of sleep can affect your immune system and reduce your ability to fight infections.

Test Your MEMORY

1. What is a disease?

2. What is illness?

3. What are nutritional deficiency diseases?

4. Write briefly about the different types of illness.

5. Name the diseases caused by the lack of Vitamin A.

6. Name the diseases caused by the lack of Vitamin D.

7. What is Vitamin B Complex?

8. Name the food sources of Vitamin C.

9. Name the diseases caused by the lack of calcium.

10. Write about the functions of iron in our body.

11. Name the diseases caused by the lack of iodine.

12. What is protein energy malnutrition?

Index

A

amnesia 18
anaemia 8, 9, 16, 18, 20, 24, 26, 28, 29
ascorbic acid 19

B

B1/Thiamine 16
B2/Riboflavin 16
B3/Niacin 16
B5/ Pantothenic acid 16
B6/ Pyridoxine 16
B12 8, 9, 16, 17, 18
beriberi 8, 18, 30
biotin 16

C

calcium 7, 9, 14, 15, 21, 22, 27, 28, 29
calories 7, 9, 27, 30
carbohydrates 7, 16, 30
collagen 19

E

epidemics 3

F

fats 7, 16, 30
fibre 7
folic acid 16, 18

G

goitre 25, 26

H

haemoglobin 23, 24

I

iodine 7, 25, 26, 29
iron 7, 8, 9, 19, 23, 24, 27, 29

K

Kwashiorkor 27, 28

M

malnutrition 7, 27, 29
Marasmus 27, 28
medicine 4, 8, 25, 29,
mental illnesses 11
micro-organisms 5, 16
minerals 7, 14, 15, 27, 30
myoglobin 23

N

night blindness 13
Nosology 4
nutrients 7, 8, 9, 27, 29, 30
nutritional deficiency diseases 7, 29

O

osteomalacia 9, 22
osteopenia 22
osteoporosis 8, 15, 20, 22

P

Pathology 4
pellagra 8, 18
Primary PEM 27
Protein-energy malnutrition (PEM) 27, 29
proteins 7, 16, 30

R

red blood cells 8, 16, 22, 23, 24
retinol 12
rickets 8, 9, 15, 22

S

Scurvy 20, 30
Secondary PEM 27, 28
starvation 7, 9, 27, 29

T

thyroid gland 25, 26
thyroxine 25

V

Vitamin A 11, 12, 13, 21, 29, 30
Vitamin B complex 16
Vitamin C 19, 20, 21, 29, 30
Vitamin D 9, 14, 15, 21
vitamins 7, 16, 30

W

water 5, 7, 16, 19, 26
World Health Organization 8

PEGASUS ENCYCLOPEDIA LIBRARY

Food and Nutrition
FOOD

Edited by: Pallabi B. Tomar, Hitesh Iplani
Managing editor: Tapasi De
Designed by: Vijesh Chahal, Anil Kumar, Rohit Kumar
Illustrated by: Suman S. Roy, Tanoy Choudhury
Colouring done by: Vinay Kumar, Kiran Kumari & Pradeep Kumar

CONTENTS

What is food? 3

Types of food 4

Food sources 8

Food chain 10

Food production through agriculture 12

Taste of food 14

Methods of preparing food 17

Food trade 23

Food poverty 24

Food allergy and intolerance 26

Food safety methods 29

Test Your Memory 31

Index 32

What is food?

Food is any substance normally eaten or drunk by living organisms. The term food also includes liquid drinks. Food is the main source of energy and of nutrition for animals and man and is usually of animal or plant origin.

The study of food is called **food science**. Historically, people obtained food from hunting and gathering, farming, ranching, and fishing, known as agriculture. Today, most of the food energy consumed by the world population is supplied by the food industry operated by multinational corporations using intensive farming and industrial agriculture methods.

Food safety and food security are monitored by agencies such as the International Association for Food Protection, World Resources Institute, World Food Programme, Food and Agriculture Organization and International Food Information Council. They address issues such as sustainability, biological diversity, climate change, nutritional economics, population growth, water supply and access to food.

Astonishing fact

During the Alaskan Klondike gold rush (1897-1898), potatoes were practically worth their weight in gold. Potatoes were so valued for their vitamin C content that miners traded gold for potatoes!

Types of food

Fast food

Fast food is any food that is quick, convenient and usually inexpensive. You can buy fast food just about anywhere that sells food and snacks. Vending machines, drive-through restaurants and 24 hour convenience stores are probably the most common places to find fast food. However, fast food is inexpensive because it is usually made with cheaper ingredients such as high fat meat, refined grains and added sugar and fats, instead of nutritious foods such as lean meats, fresh fruits and vegetables.

Fast-food outlets are take-away or take-out providers, often with a 'drive-thru' service which allows customers to order and pick up food from their cars; but most of them also have a seating area in which customers can eat the food on the premises.

Nearly from its inception, fast food has been designed to be eaten 'on the go' and often does not require traditional dominant cutlery. Common menu items at fast food outlets include fish and chips, sandwiches, pitas, hamburgers, fried chicken, French fries, chicken nuggets, tacos, pizza and ice cream.

Fortune cookies were invented in 1916 by George Jung, a Los Angeles noodle maker.

Junk food

Any food that has poor nutritional value is considered unhealthy maybe called a junk food. A food that is high in fat, sodium and sugar is known as a junk food. Junk food is easy to carry, purchase and consume. Generally, a junk food is given a very attractive appearance by adding food additives and colours to enhance flavour, texture, appearance and increasing long self life.

A junk food has little enzyme producing vitamins and minerals and contains high level of calories. When we eat these empty calorie foods, the body is required to produce its own enzymes to convert these empty calories into usable energy. This is not desired as these enzyme producing functions in our body should be reserved for the performance of vital metabolic reactions.

Since junk food is high in fats and sugars, it is responsible for obesity, dental cavities, Type 2 diabetes and heart diseases.

Foods which fall under junk food vary depending on a number of factors. Snack foods like chips, candies and so forth are generally universally agreed upon as junk food, and some people also include fast food like hamburgers, pizza and fries into the junk food category.

> McDonald's fast food chains employ over 1.5 million people around the world.

FOOD

Whole foods

Whole foods are foods that are as close to their natural or original states as possible. This means they have not been processed or refined. It also means they are free of additives, such as colourings and preservatives and have not been modified.

Fruits and vegetables are great examples of whole foods. They are unprocessed, unrefined and can be eaten without any additives or modifications. Nuts, seeds, beans, lentils and peas also make the grade. Milk and eggs can be included in this category, as can meats, poultry and fish.

One reason to choose whole foods over their processed counterparts is nutritional intake. Often, as a result of processing, important vitamins and minerals are lost and the food may become less healthy. Even things like fibre and water can be diminished through processing and refinement making the food significantly less useful for the body.

Another benefit whole foods offer over processed choices is the lack of added sugar and sodium. Obesity is a problem in some countries, a fact that is probably influenced by the added sugars in the foods we eat. Likewise, excess sodium can contribute to health problems such as high blood pressure and many processed foods are high in sodium.

> Cutting onions releases a gas which causes a stinging sensation when it comes into contact with your eyes. Your body produces tears to dilute the irritant and remove it from your eyes.

Types of food

Organic food

Organic food refers to the food items that are produced, processed and packaged without using chemicals. Organic food is increasingly becoming popular due to its perceived health benefits over conventional food. The industry is growing rapidly since the past five years and has caught the attention of farmers, manufacturers and above all, consumers.

The organic revolution is a global phenomenon witnessed in every part of the world including US, Canada, Mexico, Austria, Denmark, Finland, France, Germany, Italy, The Netherlands, Spain, Sweden, Switzerland, UK, Hungary, Poland, Australia, New Zealand, China, India, Japan, Malaysia, Singapore, Thailand, Turkey, Argentina, Brazil, Chile and South Africa. These regions are important production as well as demand centres.

Popular organic food items include organic tea, organic coffee, organic wine, organic meat, organic beef, organic milk, organic honey, organic vegetables, organic fruits, organic rice, organic corn, organic herbs, organic essential oils, organic coconut oil and organic olive oil.

> **Rice is the staple food of more than one-half of the world's population.**

Food sources

Almost all foods are of plant or animal origin. Cereal grain is a staple food that provides more food energy worldwide than any other type of crop. Maize, wheat and rice together account for 87 per cent of all grain production worldwide. Other foods not from animal or plant sources include various edible fungi, especially mushrooms. Fungi and bacteria are used in the preparation of fermented and pickled foods such as leavened bread, alcoholic drinks, cheese, pickles and yogurt.

From plants

- Grasses and their grains, including barley, cereals, couscous, corn or maize, oats, rice, rye, sugarcane, wheat, etc
- Fruits
- Herbs
- Legumes, including beans, peas, lentils, etc
- Nuts
- Seeds
- Spices
- Vegetables

Saffron, made from the dried stamens of cultivated crocus flowers is the most expensive cooking spice.

Food sources

From animals

- Dairy products, including milk
- Eggs
- Insects, including honey
- Meat, including beef, goat, horse, kangaroo, lamb, mutton, pork, veal
- Poultry, including chicken, turkey, duck, goose, pigeon or dove, ostrich, emu, guinea fowl, pheasant, quail
- Seafood, including finfish such as salmon and tilapia, and shellfish such as mollusks and crustaceans
- Snails

Astonishing fact

The colour of a chilli is no indication of its spiciness, but size usually matters; the smaller, the hotter it is.

From neither animals or plants

- Salt
- Mushrooms
- Water, including mineral water and spring water

Spring water

Food chain

Every plant and animal species, no matter how big or small, depends to some extent on another plant or animal species for its survival. It could be bees taking pollen from a flower, photosynthesis of plants, deer eating shrub leaves or lions eating the deer.

A food chain shows how energy is transferred from one living organism to another via food. It is important for us to understand how the food chain works so that we know what are the important living organisms that make up the food chain and how the ecology is balanced.

A food chain describes how energy and nutrients move through an ecosystem. At the basic level there are plants that produce the energy, then it moves up to higher-level organisms like herbivores. After that when carnivores eat the herbivores, energy is transferred from one to the other.

In the food chain, energy is transferred from one living organism through another in the form of food. There are primary producers, primary consumers, secondary consumers and decomposers- all part of the food chain.

> When honey is swallowed, it enters the blood stream within a period of 20 minutes.

Sun → Grass → Herbivore (Deer) → Carnivore (Lion)

Food chain

Herbivores

Producers are always the first link in a food chain. Producers are plants and are capable of making their own food through the process of photosynthesis. Grass is an example of a producer.

Primary consumers are the next link in a food chain. Herbivores or plant eaters are the first consumer of the energy produced by plants. A rabbit is a prime example of a primary consumer.

Secondary consumers are carnivores or meat eaters and are the third link in the food chain. They obtain energy by eating herbivores. An example of a secondary consumer is a fox. A secondary consumer can also be an omnivore, an animal that consumes plants and animals.

Decomposers are the final link in the food chain. A decomposer breaks down dead plants and animals, so they can become food for plants. Worms are decomposers.

Astonishing fact

Three quarters of fish caught are eaten. The rest is used to make things such as glue, soap, margarine and fertilizer.

This interdependence of the populations within a food chain helps to maintain the balance of plant and animal populations within a community. For example, when there are too many giraffes, there will be insufficient trees and shrubs for all of them to eat. Many giraffes will starve and die. Fewer giraffes means more time for the trees and shrubs to grow to maturity and multiply. Fewer giraffes also mean less food is available for the lions to eat and some lions will starve to death. When there are fewer lions, the giraffe population will increase.

Omnivore

Carnivore

Food production through agriculture

Civilization began with agriculture, our nomadic ancestors settled once they began to grow their own food.

Agriculture refers to the production of goods through growing of plants, animals and other life forms on land. As of 2006, 45 per cent of the world's population is employed in agriculture.

However, the relative significance of farming has dropped since the beginning of industrialization. Even though agriculture employs one-third of the world's population, agricultural produce accounts for less than 5 per cent of the gross world product.

Agriculture is a very important activity for the survival of human beings on this Earth. This is clearly reflected in the very basic fact that agriculture is one of the oldest activities of humankind. The term 'agriculture' includes both the cultivation of crops and the domestication of animals. It is the science of farming, which is raising crops like corn, beans, peas, soybeans and also raising animals like cows, sheep, pigs, goats and chickens.

Astonishing fact

1.5 billion cups of tea are enjoyed throughout the world every day!

Food production through agriculture

Astonishing fact

To make one kilo of honey, bees have to visit 4 million flowers, travelling a distance equal to 4 times around the Earth.

As the most profound resource, agriculture provides food, clothing and shelter to us. With the spread of knowledge of the most advanced implements, there has been immense progress in the spread of agriculture, as well as agricultural output. The use of agricultural machinery, scientific methods of farming and diversification of crops have improved the overall production of agricultural crops the world over.

Agriculture is important for not only providing food but also for providing raw materials for other industries like textile, sugar, jute, vegetable oil and tobacco. Besides being an occupation for people, agriculture is also a way of living.

Most of the world's customs and cultures revolve around agriculture. A number of festivals and holidays around the world are in conjunction with reaping or harvesting or any other aspect of farming. It increases the supply of food and tax revenue to the government.

FOOD

Taste of food

Taste is the sensing of flavour in food and other material that is ingested. Taste is possible because chemicals stimulate receptors on the tongue, the taste buds. How something tastes can tell an individual whether that something is food or inedible, like cardboard and toxic substances often have a disdainful taste, something that some animals and insects use to their advantage.

The four common types of taste are the basic sweet, salty, bitter and sour sensations. However, a fifth taste was recently added to the list, savoury (also known as meaty or umami).

The bumpy texture of the tongue, which is often visible, is caused by the taste buds (sometimes called **gustatory cells**). The bumps are actually called papillae and within them are microvilli, microscopic hairs that send messages to the nervous system. These nerve endings are stimulated by chemicals. The average person has thousands (approximately 10,000) of these taste receptors on their tongue and the taste that is tasted depends entirely on which chemical signal is sent.

Astonishing fact

Bananas are the world's most popular fruit after tomatoes.

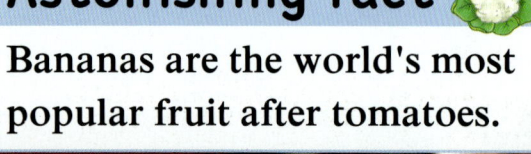

Taste of food

Sweetness

Sweetness is one of the five basic tastes and is almost universally regarded as a pleasurable experience. Foods rich in simple carbohydrates such as sugar are those most commonly associated with sweetness, although there are other natural and artificial compounds that are sweet at much lower concentrations, allowing their use as non-caloric sugar substitutes.

Sweet taste is also found in milk and milk products (like butter, ghee and cream), most grains (especially wheat, rice, and barley), many legumes (like beans and lentils), sweet fruits (such as bananas and mangos) and certain cooked vegetables (such as carrots, sweet potatoes and beets).

Saltiness

Saltiness is a taste produced by the presence of sodium chloride (and to a lesser degree other salts). The ions of salt, especially sodium can pass directly through ion channels in the tongue, leading to an action potential. It is found in any salt (such as sea salt and rock salt), sea vegetables (like seaweed and kelp), and foods to which large amounts of salt are added (like nuts, chips and pickles).

> 60 million tons of tomatoes and 44 million tons of bananas are produced annually. Apples are the third most popular (36 million tons) fruit which is produced, then oranges (34 million tons) and then watermelons (22 million tons).

FOOD

Sourness

Sour is a basic taste that is considered agreeable only in small amounts. An aversive taste, it wards off the ingestion of harmful substances. It is commonly found in citrus fruits (such as lemon and limes), sour milk products (like yogurt, cheese and sour cream) and fermented substances (including wine, vinegar, pickles, sauerkraut and soy sauce).

Bitterness

Bitterness is perceived by many to be unpleasant. It is found in green leafy vegetables (such as spinach, kale and green cabbage), other vegetables (including zucchini and eggplant), herbs and spices (like turmeric, fenugreek and dandelion root), coffee, tea and certain fruits (such as grapefruits, olives, and bitter melon). While bitter taste is often not appealing alone, it stimulates the appetite and helps bring out the flavour of the other tastes.

Savouriness (Umami)

Umami is a Japanese word meaning 'savoury' or 'meaty' and thus applies to

the sensation of savouriness. Umami is an appetitive taste facilitating ingestion of protein-rich food and it is variously described as a savoury, brothy or meaty taste. Umami can be tasted in cheese and soy sauce and while also found in many other fermented and aged foods this taste is also present in tomatoes, grains and beans.

Astonishing fact

There are more than 10,000 varieties of tomatoes!

Methods of preparing food

Baking

Baking is simply a cooking technique in which dry heat is applied to a food product in a closed environment, such as an oven. During the baking process, consistent temperature is maintained to ensure proper browning and doneness.

Baking is one of the most versatile of cooking techniques because it can achieve a variety of unique results-puffy soufflés, crispy baked potatoes, creamy casseroles and delicate pastries-using one simple but exacting method. Put together your ingredients in the right proportions, select the appropriate oven temperature and maintain that temperature consistently throughout the baking process and your finished result should be perfect.

Astonishing fact
The can opener was invented 48 years after cans were introduced.

Barbecuing

Nothing beats the deep, rich flavour of good barbecue. Barbecue refers to the slow, indirect cooking of meats over a wood, charcoal or gas flame. The meat is often seasoned with rubs, sauces or mops. This same method is known as barbie in Australia and braai in South Africa. Asian barbecue on the other hand, uses thinly sliced meat and seafood, often highly seasoned, that is quick-cooked on a hot grill or a searing hotplate.

FOOD

Braising

Braising is a form of moist-heat cooking in which the item to be cooked is partially covered with liquid and then simmered slowly at a low temperature. Braising is a good way to cook the tougher cuts of meat such as shank, shoulder and round. Long, slow simmering breaks down the connective tissue in the meat. However, delicate foods such as fish and seafood can also be braised. Cooking time is simply shorter.

The liquid used as a braising medium is usually water or stock, but wine, beer or tomatoes are sometimes used. And other ingredients such and onions, carrots or potatoes are often added to impart different flavours.

Astonishing fact
Over the last 40 years food production actually increased faster than population.

Frying

Frying is the cooking of food with oil. Due to the higher temperature of oil compared with water-based cooking, the cooking time is much shorter.

Deep frying is a frying process where the food is completely immersed in oil. Stir frying is a way of quick cooking foods with a small amount of oil over high heat. This ingenious cooking method from the East preserves the flavour, freshness and nutrients of a dish's ingredients. Since cooking goes so quickly, the main thing to remember when stir frying is to have all your ingredients prepared and close at hand before you begin cooking.

Methods of preparing food

Astonishing fact
In the Middle Ages, sugar was a treasured luxury costing 9 times as much as milk.

Grilling

Grilling is the quick cooking of meat, fish or vegetables over intense heat. It is a form of cooking that involves dry heat applied to the surface of food, commonly from above or below. Grilling usually involves quite a lot of direct, radiant heat and tends to be used for cooking quickly meat that has already been cut into slices. Food to be grilled is cooked on a grill (an open wire grid with a heat source above or below), a grill pan (similar to a frying pan, but with raised ridges to mimic the wires of an open grill) or griddle (a flat plate heated from below).

Items to be grilled can be flavoured in a marinade or seasoned with a rub (a type of marinade-wet or dry). They can be basted while cooking with any variety of flavourful sauces, or topped with a flavoured butter before serving.

Poaching

Poaching is a great way of cooking food that cuts fat, enhances flavour and keeps delicate foods from turning tough. This simple cooking method involves slow simmering eggs, meat, poultry, fish, seafood or fruit in a flavourful liquid just long enough to cook it through.

FOOD

Astonishing fact
Approximately one billion snails are served in restaurants annually.

Preserving

In days before the refrigerator, the only way to get food to last through lean times was through various methods of preservation. Drying, curing, brining, pickling, fermenting and smoking are just some of the ways used for preserving food. These methods have all survived modernization simply because they make food so tasty.

Roasting

With roasting, direct heat is applied to the food. The heat seals the outside part of the food and the juice inside the food cooks the food. Roasting is mainly used when cooking fleshy food like fish, meat or chicken. When heat is applied to the outer covering of the food, it seals it up thereby trapping all the juices inside the food. The action of direct heating, heats up the juices inside the food, which then cooks the food. Again there is very little nutrient lost and the flavour is not spoilt. Food is frequently rotated over the spit so that there is even heating applied to all parts of the food. This is done so that heat is applied evenly to the food to make it get cooked properly.

Methods of preparing food

Sautéing

Sautéing is a form of cooking that uses a very hot pan and a small amount of fat to cook the food very quickly. Sautéing browns the food's surface as it cooks and develops complex flavours and aromas. It generally consists of searing portion-sized cuts of meat or fish in hot oil on both sides to brown. The meat or fish is then removed, and the remaining bits and juices in the pan are incorporated into either a pre-made sauce or the sauce is made directly in the pan.

Steaming

Steaming involves suspending food over simmering or boiling water and cooking it with the resulting steam. Steaming as a method is valued for the fact that it preserves vitamins and minerals in the food that might otherwise be washed away with boiling. It is also a way to cut back on fat, since none is needed.

Astonishing fact

Tea is said to have been discovered in 2737 BC by a Chinese emperor when some tea leaves accidentally blew into a pot of boiling water.

The simplest way to steam food is to place a steaming basket in a saucepan over about an inch or two of water. Place the food to be steamed in the basket, cover it with a lid and bring the water to a slow boil. Most foods will finish cooking in anywhere from 5 to 10 minutes.

Many vegetables are ideal for steaming, as are fillets of fish and many types of shellfish. Tougher cuts of meat are not as good for steaming since they need more cooking time to get tender. But chicken breasts do well.

21

FOOD

Stewing

When chunks of meat, seafood or vegetables are slow-simmered in a flavourful liquid brew, the result is a warming, comforting dish called a stew. Slow, moist cooking is the best way to tenderize tough cuts of meat. Stews are also a great way to use up leftovers.

In the stewing method food is cooked using a lot of liquid. Different kinds of vegetables are chopped, diced or cubed and added to the pot. Sometimes pieces of selected meat, fish or chicken is also chopped and added to the stew. The liquid is slightly thickened and stewed food is served in that manner. This method is also used when preparing fruits that are going to be served as desserts. With this cooking method, every food is cooked together at the same time in one pot. The flavour, colours, shapes and textures of the different vegetables that are used, makes stewing a handy method of cooking.

Astonishing fact

An onion, apple and potato all have the same taste. The differences in flavour are caused by their smell.

Boiling

This is the most common method of cooking and is also the simplest. With this method of cooking, enough water is added to food and it is then cooked over the fire. The action of the heated water makes the food to get cooked. The liquid is usually thrown away after the food is cooked. In the case of cooking rice, all the water is absorbed by the rice grains to get it cooked. During the heating process, the nutrients can get lost or destroyed and the flavour can be reduced with this method of cooking.

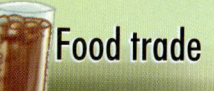

Food trade

Food is now traded on a global basis. The variety and availability of food is no longer restricted by the diversity of locally grown food or the limitations of the local growing season. Between 1961 and 1999 there has been a 400 per cent increase in worldwide food exports. Some countries are now economically dependent on food exports, which in some cases account for over 80 per cent of all exports.

Food is an essential part of our lives, which is why the way it is grown, processed and transported is worth understanding and improving. Broadly, the food industry comprises a complex network of activities pertaining to the supply, consumption and catering of food products and services across the world. Finished food products and partially prepared 'instant' food packets are also a part of the food industry. The food industry employs a massive number of skilled and unskilled workers. In 2006 alone, the food industry accounted for over 1.5 million jobs in the US and 4 million jobs in Europe.

A number of factors heighten the demand in the global food industry such as the population levels, wealth distribution, health awareness (organic food) and types of varied lifestyles. The people responsible for the food supply take many things into account like the quality of the supply chain, level of competition in the industry and the composition of the target consumers.

The world's first chocolate candy was produced in 1828 by Dutch chocolate-maker Conrad J. Van Houten.

23

Food poverty

Food poverty can be defined as the 'inability to obtain healthy affordable food'. This maybe because people lack shops in their area or have trouble reaching them. Other factors influencing food access are the availability of a range of healthy goods in local shops, income, transport, fear of crime, knowledge about what constitutes a healthy diet and the skills to create healthy meals.

Due to this complex mix of factors, people on low incomes have the lowest intakes of fruit and vegetables and are far more likely to suffer from diet-related diseases such as cancer, diabetes, obesity and coronary heart disease. Food poverty can also be about an overabundance of 'junk' food as well as a lack of healthy food.

Households in food poverty do not have enough food to meet the energy and nutrient needs of all of their members. Depending on patterns of food distribution within a household at least one member of a food-poor household is always hungry but, potentially, all members are.

Some households live under conditions of chronic or seasonal food poverty. Other households are pushed into food poverty because of changes in area food availability and/or in their own ability to secure entitlement to food.

Astonishing fact

There are more than 100 varieties of thyme.

Food poverty

The first volume of recipes was published in 62 A.D. by the Roman Apicius. Titled De Re Coquinaria, it described the feasts enjoyed by the Emperor Claudius.

About 25,000 people die every day of hunger or hunger-related causes, according to the United Nations. Unfortunately, it is children who die most often.

Yet there is plenty of food in the world for everyone. The problem is that hungry people are trapped in severe poverty. They lack the money to buy enough food to nourish themselves. Being constantly malnourished, they become weaker and often sick. This makes them increasingly less able to work, which then makes them even poorer and hungrier. This downward spiral often continues until death occurs for them and their families.

There are effective programs to break this spiral. For adults, there are 'food for work' programs where the adults are paid with food to build schools, dig wells, make roads, etc. This does both— nourishes them and builds infrastructure to end the poverty. For children, there are 'food for education' programs where the children are provided with food when they attend school. Their education will help them to escape from hunger and global poverty.

Food allergy and intolerance

A **food allergy** is a term that health experts reserve for any abnormal reaction by the body's disease-fighting immune system to an otherwise harmless food or component of food.

When a reaction to a food occurs that does not involve the body's immune system, it is called food intolerance. This is not a food allergy.

Food intolerance stems from problems with digestion or metabolism. Usually the problem involves a defect or deficiency in an enzyme in the body, a chemical necessary for the breakdown or absorption of a particular food deficiency.

Food allergies occur when the immune system attacks certain proteins in certain foods. The substances in the food that trigger this immune-system response, are called **allergens**.

The immune system is a complex network of cells and molecules that help defend the body against foreign substances. When a properly functioning immune system detects a foreign substance, it responds to this threat by producing proteins called antibodies against the invaders. The antibodies will recognize and attack this foreign substance when they next encounter it. This 'battle' is what causes the allergy symptoms.

Typical symptoms of food allergy includes, swelling of face, lips and tongue, hives, dizziness, breathlessness, tingling sensation or fainting. In general, food allergy is experienced by 2 per cent of adults and 6 per cent of children. The most common food allergies are peanuts, tree nuts (such as walnuts, pecans and almonds), fish and shellfish, milk, eggs, soy products and wheat.

Astonishing fact

When ketchup was originally developed by the Chinese in 1690, it contained no tomatoes. It was made out of pickled fish, shellfish and spices.

Food intolerance is a digestive system response rather than an immune system response. It occurs when something in a food irritates a person's digestive system or when a person is unable to properly digest or breakdown the food. Intolerance to lactose, which is found in milk and other dairy products is the most common food intolerance.

Lactose intolerance is the most common type of food intolerance experienced by many. Enzyme lactase is deficient in such individuals. Lactase is essential for lactose (milk sugar) breakdown in milk and milk products. Symptoms of lactose intolerance include bloating, diarrhoea, abdominal discomfort and gas. Differentiating food intolerance from food allergy is important to prevent recurrence. Food allergies fail to allow even a miniscule amount of the food, whereas, small portions of the particular food can be eaten in case of food intolerance.

There are many factors that may contribute to food intolerance. In some cases, as with lactose intolerance, the person lacks the chemicals called enzymes necessary to properly digest certain proteins found in food. Also common are intolerances to some chemical ingredients added to food to provide colour, enhance taste, and protect against the growth of bacteria.

Astonishing fact

In South Africa, termites are often roasted and eaten by the handful like popcorn!

FOOD

Food allergies affect about 2 to 4 per cent of adults and 6 to 8 per cent of children. Food intolerances are much more common. In fact, nearly everyone at one time has had an unpleasant reaction to something they ate. Some people have specific food intolerances.

Food allergies can be triggered by even a small amount of the food and occur every time the food is consumed. People with food allergies are generally advised to avoid the offending foods completely. On the other hand, food intolerances often are dose related.

People with food intolerance may not have symptoms unless they eat a large portion of the food or eat the food frequently. For example, a person with lactose intolerance maybe able to drink milk in coffee or a single glass of milk, but becomes sick if he or she drinks several glasses of milk.

Food allergies and intolerances are also different from food poisoning, which generally results from spoiled or tainted food and affects more than one person eating the food.

India is the world's largest producer of turmeric powder as well as the world's largest consumer of the powder.

Food safety methods

Food safety is the utilization of various resources and strategies to ensure that all types of foods are properly stored, prepared and preserved so they are safe for consumption. Practicing this level of food sanitation begins with the purchase or acquisition of different food items and ends with the proper storage of leftovers for future use. Many of the food safety methods used in restaurants can also be employed at home. Here are some examples.

One of the most important aspects of practicing food safety involves preventing foods from becoming contaminated. Making sure foods are stored properly goes a long way in avoiding any type of food contamination. Meat and vegetables should be placed in airtight containers and placed in a freezer. Items such as flour, sugar, cornmeal and spices should also be stored in containers that provide an effective barrier to airborne bacteria, and can be stored in pantries when not in active use.

Basic kitchen sanitation guidelines are also an important component of any food safety strategy. Preparation counters should be disinfected regularly. Cutting boards should also be cleaned after each use. Knives, spatulas, pans, pots and other tools used in the preparation of food should be washed in hot soapy water or run through a dishwasher. This can help minimize the opportunity for food residue to breed bacteria that could contaminate food the next time the tools are used.

Astonishing fact

There are more than 500 avocado varieties.

Care should also be taken to wash all fresh fruits and vegetables thoroughly before initiating any type of food preparation. This simple process will help remove a significant amount of germs and bacteria reducing the chances of some type of food borne illness from developing. With foods that are peeled, washing helps to prevent the transfer of contaminants from the peel to the knife and ultimately to the food itself.

Leftovers should be placed in airtight containers and placed into the refrigerator or freezer immediately after a meal. This helps to preserve the leftovers for use in other dishes at a later date by maintaining the quality of the food and protecting it from possible contamination. Doing so makes it possible to utilize leftover corn, potatoes and other vegetables in soups or casseroles at a later date, with no worries about possible contamination.

Practicing food safety not only helps to maintain good health, but can also help save money. Storing food properly, as well as making sure to prepare food in a clean environment, means that there is less chance of food spoiling and being thrown out.

Unsafe food causes many acute and life-long diseases, ranging from diarrhoeal diseases to various forms of cancer. WHO estimates that food borne and waterborne diarrhoeal diseases taken together kill about 2.2 million people annually.

Astonishing fact

Archaeologists have evidence of people eating apples as far back as 6500 B.C.

Test Your MEMORY

1. What is food?

2. Name the types of food.

3. Name the food sources.

4. What is a food chain?

5. Write briefly about food production through agriculture.

6. What are the different tastes of food?

7. What are the various methods for the preparation of food?

8. What is food trade?

9. What is food poverty?

10. What is food allergy?

11. What is food intolerance?

12. Write some food safety methods.

FOOD

Index

A
agriculture 3, 12, 13
allergens 26
antibodies 26

B
baking 17
barbecuing 17
bitter 14, 16
boiling 21, 22
braising 18

C
carnivores 10, 11

D
decomposers 10, 11
deep frying 18

E
ecology 10
ecosystem 10

F
fast food 4, 5
fibre 6
food allergy 26, 27
food chain 10, 11
food intolerance 26, 27
food poisoning 28
food poverty 24
food safety 3, 29, 30
food science 3

G
fruits 4, 6, 7, 8, 15, 16, 22, 30
frying 18, 19

G
grilling 19

H
herbivores 10, 11

I
immune system 26, 27

J
junk food 5, 24

L
lactose intolerance 27, 28

M
minerals 5, 6, 21

N
nutrition 3

O
obesity 5, 6, 24
organic food 7, 23

P
poaching 19
preserving 20
primary 10, 11
primary consumers 10

processing 6
producers 10, 11

R
refinement 6
roasting 20

S
salty 14
sautéing 21
secondary consumers 10, 11
sour 14, 16
steaming 21
stewing 22
stir frying 18
sweet 14, 15

T
taste 14, 15, 16, 22, 27
taste buds 14

U
umami 14, 16

V
vegetables 4, 6, 7, 8, 15, 16, 19, 21, 22, 24, 29, 30
vitamins 5, 6, 21

W
water 3, 6, 9, 18, 21, 22, 29
whole foods 6

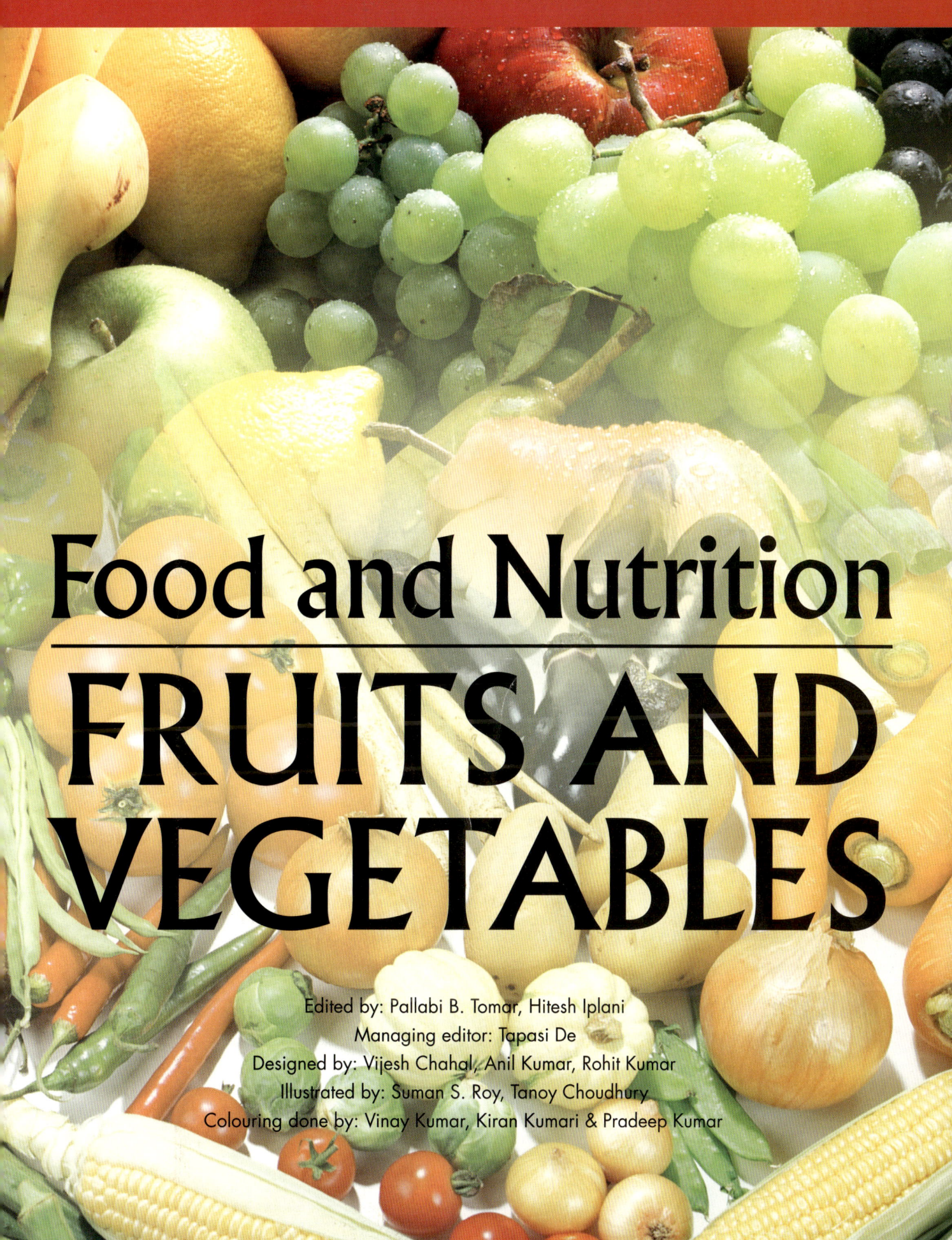

PEGASUS ENCYCLOPEDIA LIBRARY

Food and Nutrition
FRUITS AND VEGETABLES

Edited by: Pallabi B. Tomar, Hitesh Iplani
Managing editor: Tapasi De
Designed by: Vijesh Chahal, Anil Kumar, Rohit Kumar
Illustrated by: Suman S. Roy, Tanoy Choudhury
Colouring done by: Vinay Kumar, Kiran Kumari & Pradeep Kumar

CONTENTS

What are fruits? 3

Types of fruits 4

Uses of fruits 6

Nutritional value of fruits 8

What are vegetables? 10

Types of vegetables 11

Benefits of vegetables 14

Nutritional value of vegetables 16

Fruits vs. vegetables 18

Importance of fruits and vegetables 20

Some exotic fruits and vegetables 22

Test Your Memory 31

Index 32

What are fruits?

Fruits are the ripened seed-bearing part of a plant which is fleshy and edible. In other words, a 'fruit' is any fleshy material covering a seed or seeds. Most fruits from a horticultural perspective are grown on a woody plant, with the exception of strawberries.

Fruit has a different meaning in different contexts. In botanical terms, fruit refers to a ripened ovary of a flowering plant. In some cases, fruit refers to the ripened ovary with its surrounding tissues.

Fruit, in food preparation, refers to the sweet, fleshy and edible parts of a plant such as oranges, plums and apples. Some fruits, including tomato, cucumber, pumpkin, squash, beans, corn, peas and sweet pepper, are considered vegetables by those involved in food preparation. In the strictest culinary sense, fruit is any sweet tasting plant product associated with seed or seeds.

Astonishing fact

Squash and pumpkins have been cultivated for more than 9,000 years.

Types of fruits

Botanists have defined fruits as ripened ovaries along with their contents and adhering accessory structures. Fruits are produced from flowers on the plants and trees. Flowers are pollinated and these fertilized flowers turn into fruits. The ovule turns to seeds, the petals fall off and the ovary surrounding the ovule starts swelling. The three basic types of fruits are:

1) Simple fruit

2) Aggregate fruit

3) Multiple fruit

Simple Fruit

Simple fruits are those fruits that develop from a single ovary in a single flower. They can be either dry or fleshy.

Dry fruits could be dehiscent fruit which open to discharge seeds or indehiscent fruit which do not do so.

Examples of dry simple fruits include legumes (pea, bean and peanut), capsules (Brazil nut), fibrous drupe (coconut and walnut), carrot, utricle (beets), silique as in radish and others.

Examples of fleshy simple fruits include pome (accessory fruits like apple, pear, rosehip) and berry (redcurrant, gooseberry, tomato and avocado), false berry (banana and cranberry) or stone fruit (plum, cherry, peach, apricot and olive).

Astonishing fact

Star fruit seeds are highly toxic and are used to make insecticide.

Types of fruits

Aggregate Fruit

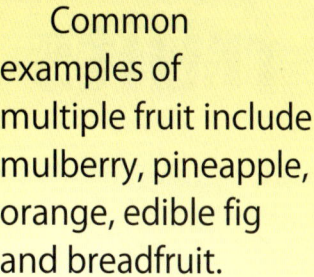

An aggregate fruit develops from a flower with numerous simple pistils. An example is the raspberry, whose simple fruits are termed drupelets because each is like a small drupe (a fleshy fruit with thin skin with a seed) attached to the receptacle. In some bramble fruits (such as blackberry), the receptacle is elongate and part of the ripe fruit, making the blackberry an aggregate-accessory fruit. The strawberry is also an aggregate-accessory fruit, only one in which, the seeds are contained in achenes (a small, dry one-seeded fruit). In all these examples, the fruit develops from a single flower with numerous pistils.

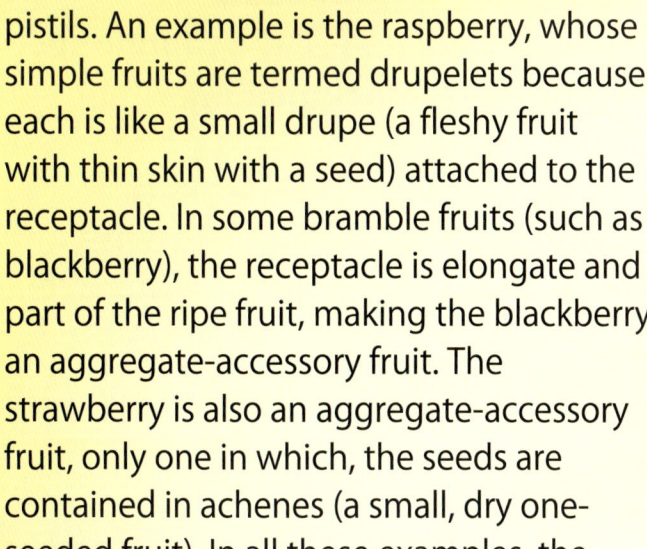

Multiple Fruit

A fruit formed from a cluster of flowers is called a multiple fruit. Each flower produces a fruit but they eventually merge into a single mass.

Common examples of multiple fruit include mulberry, pineapple, orange, edible fig and breadfruit.

Other dry multiple fruits include sweet gum (a multiple of capsules), tulip tree (a multiple of samaras), sycamore and teasel (multiples of achenes) and magnolia (a multiple of follicles).

> Kale has been cultivated for over 2,000 years. It's a leafy cabbage like plant rich in Vitamins A and C, calcium and fibre.

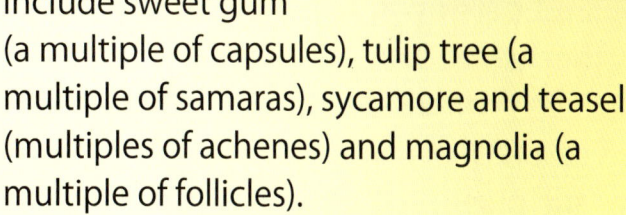

Uses of fruits

Everyone knows that fruits contain many vitamins necessary to our organism. Scientists have proved that many fruits possess qualities that protect us from many diseases.

- Fruits are one of the most important, healthy and natural foods in existence. Fruits contain a large number of naturally occurring vitamins, minerals and plant phytochemicals that help benefit health. It has also been observed that eating whole fruits or drinking their juice is best to gain the benefits rather than taking supplements to provide each nutrient separately.

- Fruits have a high fibre content that helps to control the blood glucose levels. It reduces blood cholesterol and the risk of colon cancer and other cancers.

- A balanced diet including at least five portions of fruits daily will provide all the Vitamin C that the body needs, plus many more beneficial vitamins and minerals.

In English-speaking countries, the cantaloupe is known as Rockmelon.

- Some fruits also have medicinal qualities. For e.g., Bilberry fruit has been used for diarrhoea, inflammation of the mouth and throat and to improve night vision.

Uses of fruits

Many hundreds of fruits, including fleshy fruits like apple, peach, pear, kiwifruit, watermelon and mango are commercially valuable as human food, eaten both fresh and as jams, marmalade and other preserves. Fruits are also in manufactured foods like cookies, muffins, yoghurt, ice cream, cakes and many more. Many fruits are used to make beverages, such as fruit juices (orange juice, apple juice, grape juice, etc.).

Many vegetables are botanical fruits, including tomato, bell pepper, eggplant, okra, squash, pumpkin, green bean, cucumber and zucchini. Olive fruit is pressed for olive oil. Spices like vanilla, paprika, allspice and black pepper are derived from berries.

As fruits have been such a major part of the human diet, different cultures have developed many different uses for various fruits that they do not depend on as being edible. Many dry fruits are used as decorations or in dried flower arrangements, such as unicorn plant, lotus, wheat, annual honesty and milkweed. Osage orange fruits are used to repel cockroaches. Bayberry fruits provide a wax often used to make candles. Dried gourds are used as decorations, water jugs, bird houses, musical instruments, cups and dishes. Coir is a fibre from the fruit of coconut that is used for doormats, brushes, mattresses, floor tiles, sacking, insulation and as a growing medium for container plants.

Did you know that one-third of the world's pineapples comes from Hawaii.

FRUITS AND VEGETABLES

Nutritional value of fruits

The nutritional value of fruit is partly owing to the supply of good vitamins and enzymes which it delivers.

The commonest vitamin in fruit is Vitamin C and this happens to be a particularly important vitamin because our bodies neither store nor manufacture it. Vitamin C protects against heart disease and cancer.

The best fruits for Vitamin C are the citrus group consisting of oranges, lemons, grapefruit and tangerines to name a few. Other excellent sources include kiwi fruit, mangoes and papayas and many of the soft fruits such as blackcurrants and strawberries.

Vitamin A is another important vitamin for the immune system, good vision and bone growth. It also helps regulate some hormones and promotes healthy teeth and hair. In fruit it generally turns up as beta carotene which the body then uses to make Vitamin A. Fruits of a deep yellow or orange colour are usually good sources of beta carotene.

A related vitamin is lycopene which is found in red coloured fruits such as tomatoes, guavas, watermelons, pink grapefruit and chillies. Lycopene has an important role in protecting us against cancers and heart disease. It is a powerful antioxidant.

Bell peppers are usually sold green, but they can also be red, purple or yellow.

Nutritional value of fruits

Astonishing fact

A hornworm can eat an entire tomato plant by itself in one day!

Another nutritional value of fruit is that it is a rich source of essential minerals. Fresh fruits supply minerals such as potassium and magnesium, iron and calcium.

Potassium helps the body to cleanse itself of impurities and also helps maintain a powerful energy system. One of the symptoms of potassium deficiency is chronic fatigue.

Good sources of potassium include bananas, blackberries, oranges and tomatoes. Avocados are incredibly rich in both potassium and Vitamin A.

Other minerals which are commonly found in fruits include calcium, magnesium and phosphorus. Calcium is a very important mineral because it is needed for healthy bone development and maintenance. Blackberries, strawberries, oranges, kiwi fruit and tomatoes are all relatively rich in calcium.

Iron is another essential mineral which is commonly found in fruit. Strawberries, blackberries, kiwi, tomatoes, grapes and bananas are all good sources of iron.

What are vegetables?

Vegetable is a nutritional and culinary term denoting any part of a plant that is commonly consumed by humans as food, but is not regarded as a culinary fruit, nut, herb, spice or grain. In common usage, vegetables include the leaves (e.g. lettuce), stems (asparagus), roots (carrot) and flowers (broccoli) of various plants. But the term can also encompass non-sweet fruits such as seed-pods (beans), cucumbers, squashes, pumpkins, tomatoes, avocadoes, green peppers, etc., as well as fleshy, immature seeds such as those of maize, peas or beans.

Commercial production of vegetables is a branch of horticulture called olericulture.

Some vegetables can be consumed raw, some maybe eaten raw or cooked, and some must be cooked in order to be edible. Vegetables are most often cooked in savoury or salty dishes. However, a few vegetables are often used in desserts and other sweet dishes, such as rhubarb pie and carrot cake.

White potatoes were first cultivated by local Indians in the Andes Mountains of South America.

Types of vegetables

Bulb vegetables

Bulb vegetables are those variety of vegetables that are not eaten directly, rather, they are used in food dishes to enhance the flavour of the food. Most of the bulb vegetables are structured in the shape of a bulb, wherein all its nutrients are stored. The nutrients provided by these vegetables are immense as they are believed to be essential to gain healthy skin and eyes, and also for the proper functioning of the central nervous system. The most known bulb vegetables are onion, chive, spring onion and garlic.

Fruit vegetables

Fruit vegetables are so called because botanically they fulfil the definition of fruits, but are used as vegetables by human beings. They are considered to be fruits because in the scientific sense of the term, fruits are those that carry the seeds of the plant. So tomatoes, cucumber, etc., which are consumed as vegetables are actually fruits because they have seeds in them. Some examples are the Avocado, Bell Pepper (capsicum), Bitter Melon, Eggplant (aubergine), Pumpkin, etc.

Flowering or Inflorescent vegetables

Flowering vegetables are so called because they have the shape of flowers. They are usually small in size and appear like many flower buds clustered together. Along with essential nutrients, flowering vegetables also bear some phytochemicals (biologically active compounds found in plants) which help in preventing the production of cancerous cells. For this reason, these vegetables are called functional vegetables. Some examples are the Artichoke, Bok Choy, Broccoli, Cauliflower, etc.

FRUITS AND VEGETABLES

Green leafy vegetables

Nutritionists have declared that it is extremely important to make green leafy vegetables a part of one's daily diet. These vegetables include a whole lot of vitamins that are required to remain fit and also to prevent some diseases and health problems. Dark green vegetables also known as pot herbs or just green vegetables, contain not only Vitamins D, A, E and K but are also rich in fibre which aids in cleansing the digestive tract. They also contain potassium, iron, magnesium, calcium, folic acid and certain phytochemicals that are important for the proper functioning of the body. Consuming green leafy vegetables everyday decreases the risk of diseases like high blood pressure, diabetes, cancer, heart diseases, etc. Some examples are the Amaranth, Arugula, Brussels Sprout, Cabbage, Celery, Lettuce, etc.

Mushrooms

Mushrooms are also considered as a type of vegetables, though they do not have stems, branches, roots, leaves or flowers. Actually, mushrooms are categorized as fungi as they are found on organic substances. However, they are included in the diet of many people across the world and are a good source of Vitamin E. Out of the 50,000 mushrooms, only twenty can be eaten!

Podded vegetables

Podded vegetables, popularly known as legumes, are seeds that are found inside two-side pods. They include all the varieties of beans, peas and lentils. When these foods are mature and dried, they have the highest food value of all the vegetables. Some examples are the Adzuki Bean, Black-eyed Pea, Chickpea, Common Bean, Drumstick, Green Bean (French beans), etc.

One cup of shredded coconut is a good source of both iron and copper.

Types of vegetables

Root vegetables

Root vegetables are those that are grown under the soil and possess nutrients that they gain from the soil. Along with vitamins and complex carbohydrates, the most special nutrient that is present in the root vegetables is the phytonutreints. It is the phytonutrients that adds colour to the vegetables and the darker the colour of the vegetable, more are the health benefits. Some examples are Beetroot, Black Cumin, Carrot, Cassava, Ginger, Parsley, Potato, Radish, etc.

> Cabbage can be stored in a plastic bag in the refrigerator's vegetable drawer for about two weeks.

Sea vegetables

Sea vegetables, popularly known as seaweeds, are those vegetables that are found under the sea. These vegetables which are found in marine salt waters and also in fresh water lakes and seas, are said to be the most nutritious amongst the different types of vegetables. Sea vegetables are very low in calories and the rich mineral content found in them are taken from the sea. Along with proteins, fibres and calcium, seaweeds also possess the richness of vitamins, iron and essential fatty acids.

Stalk or Stem vegetables

Stalk vegetables are those that have stems which can be consumed. Some of the most popular stem vegetables include asparagus, celery, fennel, etc. These vegetables can be used to make a variety of dishes and are usually served with pasta, sandwiches, soups, etc. Along with being delicious, stalk vegetables possess minerals, vitamins and antioxidants.

Benefits of vegetables

There are numerous health benefits of vegetables which make them a very important part of the human diet. Eating between four and eight one cup servings a day confers a number of benefits which cannot be obtained from other food sources.

Vegetables contain a number of vitamins and minerals which are beneficial to the human diet. Things like potassium, Vitamin C, folate and Vitamin A, among many others, can be found in abundance in vegetables. These Vitamins and minerals are needed by the body on a daily basis, and they also help the body stay healthy so that it can prevent or cope with disease and injury. Pregnant women and people with certain chronic diseases also appear to benefit from an increased intake of dietary minerals and vitamins.

Astonishing fact

There are more than five hundred varieties of onions. All of them produce tears—the older the onion, the more sulphuric compound it contains—hence, more tears!

Vegetables are low in fat and calories, a good source of dietary fibre and provide us with extra energy. All these features help control weight effectively. Being low in calories enables us to eat lots of vegetables without consuming excess energy, the high fibre content also helps fill the stomach faster limiting the total amount of food consumed. The presence of many vitamins and other chemicals in vegetables supply the body with nutrients necessary to boost energy production within the muscle cells. This gives us a natural feeling of vitality and the energy to become more active helping to burn more energy each day.

Benefits of vegetables

Studies have also suggested that eating whole foods appears to be more beneficial than consuming supplements. The health benefits of vegetables cannot be replaced by eating vitamins, because vegetables have complex trace compounds which cannot be copied. Also vegetables themselves help the body metabolize useful vitamins and minerals.

Vegetables are also high in fibre, which can reduce the risk of developing cardiovascular diseases and some cancers while regulating digestion. The health benefits of vegetables can be obtained from raw or cooked vegetables, with frozen vegetables being a good option when fresh vegetables are not available.

While eating vegetables, it is a good idea to eat a variety of different colours. Vegetables of different colours have varying levels of vitamins and minerals and by eating a range of colours, people can ensure that they get the full array of nutrients they need. Carrots, for example, are high in Vitamin A, while dark leafy greens have lots of calcium. Carrots or broccoli alone will not provide complete nutrition.

Of all grapefruit varieties, red and pink grapefruit contain the highest amounts of Vitamin A. Grapefruit is also an excellent source of Vitamin C.

FRUITS AND VEGETABLES

Astonishing fact

Many years ago, before the invention of canteens, explorers would use watermelons to carry their water.

Nutritional value of vegetables

Vegetables are important protective food and highly beneficial for the maintenance of health and prevention of disease. They contain valuable food ingredients which can be successfully utilized to build up and repair the body.

Many vegetables contain a substance called **carotene** which is changed to vitamin A in the body. Vitamin A is necessary for normal growth and vitality, for good eyesight and healthy skin and for protection against diseases; especially of the respiratory tract. A deficiency of this vitamin causes eye infection, poor vision, night blindness, frequent colds, lack of appetite and skin disorders. Generally, coloured vegetables such as green leafy vegetables, carrot, papaya, tomatoes and yellow pumpkin are rich sources of carotene.

Several leafy vegetables like fenugreek leaves, turnip greens and beet greens contain riboflavin (Vitamin B2), a member of Vitamin B-Complex. This vitamin is essential for the growth and general health of eyes, skin, nails and hair. Its deficiency causes cracking of the corner of mouth and eczema.

Vitamin C (ascorbic acid) is present in good amount in many vegetables such as bitter gourd, tomatoes, cabbage and leafy vegetables like spinach, broccoli and drumstick leaves. Vitamin C is essential for normal growth and maintenance of body tissues, especially of the joints, bones, teeth and gums and protection against infection.

Calcium is a highly soluble mineral. Phosphorus, iron, magnesium, copper and potassium present in the vegetables maintain the acid-base balance of the hydrogen concentration of the body tissues. They are helpful in the absorption of vitamins, proteins, fats and carbohydrates of the food. They are also helpful in throwing out excess liquid and salt from our body.

Two important minerals, calcium and iron found in vegetables are very useful. Calcium is essential for strong bones and teeth. Iron is essential for blood formation. It is an essential constituent of haemoglobin, which helps to carry oxygen to the cells in various parts of the body. Calcium and iron can be obtained in plenty from leafy vegetables like spinach and fenugreek leaves. Carrots, bitter gourds, onions and tomatoes are also fair sources of iron.

Astonishing fact

Dried fruits are just as nutritious as fresh fruits and they are easier to carry.

Vegetables play a crucial role in the diet of human beings around the world. They are widely recommended by nutritionists and health practitioners because they are rich in vitamins and minerals. Consuming vegetables would help in preventing serious health problems like cancer, heart diseases, diabetes, etc. Eating vegetables regularly also makes a person's immune system stronger, preventing fever, common cold and infections.

Fruits vs. vegetables

A fruit is the matured ovary of a plant, which means that it contains seeds, while a vegetable is a plant part, which does not contain seeds, although some vegetables maybe used in plant reproduction.

The major fruit and vegetable difference is that fruits contain seeds, which are capable of developing into new plants and vegetables lack seeds. Even though, some of the vegetables are used in plant reproduction, they are not considered as fruits. In short, a fruit is a matured ovary of a plant and contain seeds, whereas a vegetable can be any of the edible part of a plant, which does not contain seeds. Hence, it is the presence of seeds that makes the difference in classifying a fruit. This is the reason for classifying tomatoes, cucumbers, etc. as fruits, even though, they are used as vegetables. Other 'technical' fruits are avocados, squashes, olives, pea pods, squashes and zucchini, pumpkins and peppers. Even nuts and grains are also classified as fruits.

Fruits are ripened ovary or ovaries of a plant and contain seeds. Vegetables are edible parts of a plant, other than fruits. It can be said that, while, a fruit cannot be a vegetable (as in the case of tomatoes), a vegetable cannot be a fruit. Most of the fruits contain a simple sugar called fructose, which gives the sweet taste, but, vegetables have less amounts of fructose. The sweetness of the fruits attracts animals and birds to consume them and thereby disperse the seeds.

Darker green vegetables contain more Vitamin C than lighter green vegetables.

Fruits vs. vegetables

> ## Astonishing fact
> Carrots can help you to see better in the dark. That's because carrots contain lots of Vitamin A, which helps to prevent 'night blindness'.

Fruits result from the fertilization between pollen and the 'egg' of a flower, which eventually becomes the edible part of the plant. Fruits, therefore, grow out of flowers that have been pollinated. Any other edible part of a plant other than the fruit is considered a vegetable. For example, tubers like potatoes, leaves like spinach or mint, roots like carrot or radish, shoots like asparagus and bamboo and bulbs like onion or garlic, are all considered vegetables.

The role of fruits is to bear seeds and in turn to grow more plants. Fruits are designed to separate from the plant after some time, like an apple falling off a tree or a grape falling off a vine, so that the seeds inside can find their way into the soil and grow into a new plant. A simple test to determine if something is a fruit or a vegetable is to notice whether it has seeds. If it has seeds, technically, it is most probably a fruit. That means that many foods people think of as vegetables are in fact, fruits. For example, eggplant, cucumbers, tomatoes, green peppers and even pumpkins are all fruits.

Biologically, fruits typically contain more Vitamin C than vegetables. Tomatoes and peppers both contain high amounts of vitamin C and are fruits, although both are often grouped as vegetables. Additionally, the enzymes in fruits and vegetables are different. These enzymes help break down these foods once we digest them.

Importance of fruits and vegetables

Study after study has shown that a diet rich in fresh fruits and vegetables lowers the risk of certain cancers, heart disease and other chronic diseases and conditions. Many fresh fruits and vegetables have high amounts of many antioxidant vitamins, including Vitamin A, Vitamin E and Vitamin C. In addition to their importance as source of vitamins and minerals, fruits and vegetables also provide essential dietary fibre.

The longer the fruits or vegetables wait to be sold or eaten, the more nutrients they lose.

Fruits and vegetables contain very low levels of fats, and a diet low in fat can be quite effective for long-term weight loss. In addition, fruits and vegetables contain no cholesterol, and they are lower in calories than many other types of foods.

Fruits and vegetables have a lot of advantages besides just their nutritional importance. For one thing, they taste great and add a great deal of variety to everyday meals. Fruits and vegetables come in such a wide variety of colours, textures and flavours that they can be used in virtually every meal. Those seeking to increase their consumption of fruits and vegetables should get into the habit of using fruits in salads as toppings and as garnishes.

Importance of fruits and vegetables

Fruits and vegetables are packed full with goodness and often contain a number of essential vitamins and minerals that cannot be found in other types of foods or they may contain higher levels of these nutrients than other foods.

Different coloured fruits and vegetables contain different minerals, nutrients and antioxidants. And so, it is recommended that we consume a wide variety of fruit and vegetables in order to receive the benefits from the various types.

For example, dark green leafy vegetables such as watercress, cabbage or spinach contain certain carotenoids that protect, delay and may prevent the onset of degenerative age-related eye diseases such as cataracts or macular degeneration. They are also rich in Vitamins C and E, which are both very powerful antioxidants.

This means that eating dark green vegetables daily could help to protect the body from developing cancerous cells and from suffering heart disease.

Red, orange and yellow coloured fruits and vegetables such as melon, tomatoes, carrots and apricots contain lots of Vitamins A, C and E, which all help to fight certain types of cancer and act by neutralising free radicals in the body.

Apart from containing large amounts of Vitamins A, C and E, fruits and vegetables are also rich in Vitamins B and K plus minerals such as potassium, calcium, phosphorous, manganese and iron.

Astonishing fact

If left on a tree, an orange will not become overripe even though it will change its colour back to green (from orange).

FRUITS AND VEGETABLES

Astonishing fact
Grapes are grown in all continents except one, Antarctica.

Some exotic fruits and vegetables

Passion Fruit

Passion fruit is native to Brazil and it is the edible fruit of the passion flower. In honour of the passion of Christ, early Spanish missionaries named the fruit so. It is a small round fruit with wrinkled, red, yellow or purple-brown skin and it has the size of a large egg. The yellow flesh and small black edible seeds have an intense aromatic flavour while the texture of the fruit is jelly-like and watery. The juice of this passion fruit is used in squashes, syrups, sorbets, etc. On ripening, the skin of the fruit is wrinkled and looks old. It contains nutrients like Vitamins A and C and potassium.

Lychee

The lychee is a tropical fruit about the size of a ping pong ball. The fruit is covered in a rough, pink-to-red-coloured rind. The rind is thin and brittle, and is easily peeled from the fruit. Each fruit contains a single glossy brown seed which is inedible. The seed is covered by a layer of whitish translucent, sweet flesh. The flesh has a mild flavour and a similar consistency of a grape. Depending on the variety of lychee and its growing conditions, the seed inside maybe large and oval-shaped or small, thin and somewhat triangular. The lychee is native to southern China, but is also found in India, Taiwan, Vietnam, Indonesia and the Philippines.

Passion fruit

Some exotic fruits and vegetables

Star fruit

Star Fruit

The star fruit is also known as carambola and when cut across its middle it has a five pointed star shape and thus, its name 'star fruit'. It is the fruit of the tree Averrhoa carambola, which is a native species of India, Indonesia and Sri Lanka. The flavour of this fruit is a combination of the taste of plums, pineapples and lemons. However, some people find the star fruit taste similar to the mix of papaya fruit, orange and grapefruit. One can consume the star fruit entirely. It has a waxy skin which is green when raw and golden yellow when ripe.

Kiwano Melon

Kiwano melon is an oval shaped fruit with horns on its peel. It has a bright orange and yellow skin with a pale yellow-green pulp inside. The flavour of the pulp is sweet and a bit tart with a flavour mix of bananas, lime and cucumber. Kiwano melon is native to southern and central Africa and is commonly known as an African horned melon.

Astonishing fact

There are at least 10,000 varieties of tomatoes!

Kiwano melon

Buddha's Hand

A Buddha's hand is a very strong scented, odd looking citrus fruit. Sometimes called a Buddha's hand citron, it is an ancient fruit that is not commonly thought of for its cookery uses. The flavour and scent of a Buddha's hand are similar to those of a lemon, but its appearance is very different.

The Buddha's hand is bright yellow and its long yellow 'fingers' can number from five to twenty. The Buddha's hand needs warm weather to grow and can be damaged by the cold, but also by intense heat. The citron grows on a shrub or small tree with long, irregular branches covered in thorns. Its large, oblong leaves are pale green and grow about four to six inches. Its white flowers are tinted purplish from the outside and grow in fragrant clusters.

The Buddha's hand is thought to have originated in India. Other stories claim that the fruit was used as an offering in religious ceremonies. When the fingers of the fruit are closed, they symbolize the closed praying hand. The Buddha's hand is thought to be one of the oldest known citrus fruits.

Astonishing fact

Bananas are the most popular fruit in North America. While a few kinds are commonly found in stores, there are actually more than three hundred varieties.

In China and Japan, the fruit is mainly used to scent or freshen rooms. It is also popular in fragrances and perfumes with a citrus base. The flesh of the fruit is not juicy, and the little pulp which is there, is incredibly tangy.

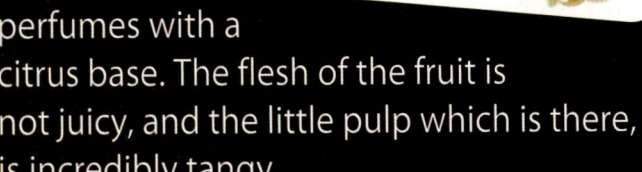

Only 5 per cent of peas grown worldwide are sold fresh.

Some exotic fruits and vegetables

Durian

Durian

Durian, an exotic fruit native to Malaysia and Indonesia and is considered to be the 'king of all fruits' in South East Asia. It is believed to have originated in Borneo and Sumatra and today besides Malaysia it is also found growing in Thailand, Southern Philippines, New Guinea, India, Sri Lanka, Vietnam and other Asian countries. Today, Thailand exports more Durian than any other country.

The durian, named for an Indonesian word meaning 'thorny,' resembles an unripe coconut with spines covering its thick, green rind. Infamous for its strangely foul smell, the flesh of this fruit is sweet and delicious.

> Eating too much carrot can turn your skin yellowish orange, especially in the palms and soles of your feet.

Rambutan

The rambutan is a medium sized tree producing a red or yellow fruit round to oval in shape. Its thin, leathery rind is covered with tubercles from each of which extends a soft, fleshy, red, pinkish or yellow spine 1/5 to 3/4 inches long. The hair like covering is responsible for the common name of the fruit, which is based on the Malay word 'rambut', meaning 'hair'.

Within the fruit is the white or rose-tinted, translucent, juicy, sweet flesh, clinging to the oblong seed. Rambutan is indigenous to the Malay Archipelago and has been widely cultivated throughout the region in Thailand, South Vietnam, Indonesia, the Philippines, India and Sri Lanka.

Rambutan

FRUITS AND VEGETABLES

Kumquat

Kumquat

A kumquat is a fruit which resembles a miniature orange. It is sometimes mistaken for a citrus fruit. The kumquat, also spelled cumquat, has a thin, sweet skin with a tart, sour flesh. The kumquat can be eaten whole, though some find its juicy centre to be too sour.

The kumquat is grown on a tree which is shrubby in appearance and usually about 2.4 - 4.5 m tall. The kumquat tree has dark, glossy green leaves and bears white flowers. The fruit itself is oval and oblong or round and ranges from golden yellow to reddish-orange in colour when ripe.

Dragon Fruit

Dragon fruits are widely consumed in Asian countries like Taiwan, Vietnam, Thailand, the Philippines, Sri Lanka and Malaysia. They are also popular in Mexico, central as well as South America. The other name for dragon fruit is Pitaya or Pitahaya.

Dragon fruit comes in three varieties—red skin with red flesh (widely considered to be the best-tasting), red skin with white flesh and yellow skin with white flesh. It roughly looks like a football. It has a leathery, leafy red skin. The fruit can weigh from 150-600 grams. Dragon fruits are mildly sweet and are best served cold. You should simply cut it in half, then scoop out the flesh with a spoon to eat it. The skin may not be eaten. The little black seeds can be eaten with the flesh, just like a kiwi fruit. The middle of the fruit is the sweetest part of the fruit.

Dragon Fruits

Placing a slice of cucumber on your eyes can cool them and reduce puffiness.

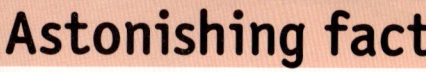

Some exotic fruits and vegetables

Astonishing fact

If you grew 100 apple trees from the seeds of one tree, they would all be different!

Jaboticaba

Jaboticaba

The Jaboticaba is also called as Brazilian Grape Tree. It is a very strange tree native to Brazil in which fruits form directly on the stem and branches. The fruit is purplish black with a white pulp. It can be eaten raw or be used to make jellies and drinks.

Jaboticaba grows on a small, bushy tree that has light brown bark with cream-coloured patches. It blossoms with small, white flowers and produces fruit at several times during the year. The fruit grows directly on the tree trunk and large branches, and not hangs off a stem. A fruit grows either on its own or in a cluster.

Broccoli Romanesco

Broccoli Romanesco is best defined by describing how it is not like a regular cauliflower. Like a cauliflower, the heads are large and tightly-formed, but the heads are of a pale lime green colour that seem to spiral upwards with pointed cones forming the spirals. It almost resembles at times a formation of sea shells. The heads are small about 4 inches in width. Romanesco retains its colour after cooking. The taste is milder and sweeter than that of the white cauliflower.

Broccoli Romanesco

FRUITS AND VEGETABLES

Artichokes

Artichokes

Artichokes are thistles that haven't blossomed yet. The artichoke grows wild in the south of Europe and is cultivated in the United States, primarily in California. The leaves proceed from the base of the stem and are long and somewhat spiny. The stem is up to 1 m high, branched, with large heads of violet-coloured (sometimes white), thistle-like flowers at the tips of the branches. The thickened receptacle (heart) and fleshy bases of the scales (leaves) of the immature flower are the portions eaten.

There are actually over 140 different varieties of artichoke plants which produce artichokes of various sizes from very small ones to ones over 4 inches wide. Green Globe is the most common variety. The Italian violetta variety is somewhat smaller.

Kohlrabi

Kohlrabi is a member of the cabbage family that is treated as a root vegetable. It is a cabbage with an enlarged, turnip-shaped stem which is referred to as a bulb. The bulb grows above the ground, just on the surface of the soil. The bulb is actually an underground stem that swells so that it grows partly above the surface.

The skin can be greenish or purplish. The plant will only produce seeds if left in the field over winter. If the bulb is left to grow too big, it becomes tough with a strong flavour. When young, it will be sweeter with a milder flavour. Kohlrabi can be harvested young within 70 days after planting from seed.

Kohlrabi

> The United States provides about one-fourth (25 per cent) of the world's total supply of fresh peaches.

Bok Choy

Bok Choy

Bok Choy, which is otherwise known as pak choi or chinese cabbage is one of the popular Chinese leafy vegetables. It is commonly used in Chinese cuisine and can be seen in soups, stir fries, steamed dishes, appetizers, etc.

Bok Choy has roundish, dark green leaves that look like crinkled spinach and crunchy, white stalks. When cooked, it has a sweet flavour and its stalks are firm.

It is a member of the cabbage family. There are several sub-varieties of Bok Choy. 'Regular' Bok Choy has white or greenish white stalks. It is normally 8 to 10 inches tall but can grow up to 20 inches.

Brussels Sprouts

A member of the crucifer family (cabbage, cauliflower, broccoli, kale) Brussels sprouts look like little miniature cabbages. The little round vegetables grow along a long tall stem. The sprouts are removed from the stem and sold fresh or frozen.

Brussels sprouts are extremely cold hardy and can even survive a first frost. Instead of forming a large single head, as their cabbage cousin does, Brussels sprouts form all along a tall stem. Approximately 20 to 40 sprouts will grow on a stem that may reach a height of 1 m.

Astonishing fact

There are more than 7,000 varieties of apples grown in the world.

Brussels sprouts

FRUITS AND VEGETABLES

Asparagus

Asparagus, a plant of the lily family native to large parts of Europe, western Asia and North Africa, is harvested for consumption when the shoots are young and tender. It is a vegetable with succulent shoots and scale-like leaves. It was known to the ancient civilization of Egypt and Rome.

It is considered a highly beneficial health food due to the presence of many vitamins, minerals and essential nutrients. Asparagus has a history of being used for medicinal purposes possibly due to its antioxidant properties. Asparagus is also good for easing off constipation, as a diuretic, as a liver and kidney detoxifier and also as an energy booster or fatigue remedy.

Asparagus

Jicama

The jicama or yam bean is a leguminous plant that is grown for its large (10-15 cm diameter) edible taproot. After removal of the thick, fibrous brown skin, the white flesh of the root can be eaten cooked or raw. Crisp, moist and slightly sweet, the flesh draws comparison with that of the apple.

By contrast to the root, the remainder of the plant is very poisonous. In particular, the rotenone-containing seeds have been used to catch fish by poisoning.

The jicama grows in frost-free climates. Native to tropical America, it is now widely known in warmer parts of China and Southeast Asia as well.

Jicama

Astonishing fact
An average strawberry has 200 seeds!

Test Your MEMORY

1. What are fruits?

2. Name the types of fruits.

3. Write some uses of fruits.

4. Write about the nutritional value of fruits.

5. What are vegetables?

6. Name the types of vegetables.

7. Write some benefits of vegetables.

8. Write about the nutritional value of vegetables.

9. Compare between fruits and vegetables.

10. Write about the importance of fruits and vegetables.

11. Name two exotic fruits.

12. Name two exotic vegetables.

Index

A
aggregate fruit 4, 5
antioxidants 13, 21
Artichokes 28
Asparagus 30

B
berry 4
Bok Choy 11, 29
Broccoli Romanesco 27
Brussels sprouts 29
Buddha's hand 24
Bulb vegetables 11

C
calories 13, 14, 20
capsules 4, 5
carotene 8, 16
cholesterol 6, 20

D
dehiscent 4
Dragon fruit 26
drupelets 5
Durian 25

E
enzymes 8, 19

F
fats 17, 20
fibre 5, 6, 7, 12, 14, 15, 20
fibrous drupe 4
flowering vegetables 11
flowers 4, 5, 10, 11, 12, 19, 24, 26, 27, 28
fruit vegetables 11

G
green leafy vegetables 12, 16, 21

I
indehiscent 4

J
Jaboticaba 27
jicama 30

K
Kiwano melon 23
Kohlrabi 28
kumquat 26

L
leaves 10, 12, 16, 17, 19, 24, 26, 28, 29, 30
legumes 4, 12
lychee 22

M
minerals 6, 9, 13, 14, 15, 17, 20, 21, 30
multiple fruit 4, 5
Mushrooms 12

O
olericulture 10
ovary 3, 4, 18
ovule 4

P
Passion fruit 22
phytochemicals 6, 11, 12
pistils 5
plants 4, 7, 10, 11, 18, 19, 28
podded vegetables 12
pollinated 4, 19
pome 4

R
Rambutan 25
roots 10, 12, 19
root vegetables 13

S
salads 20
sea vegetables 13
seeds 3, 4, 5, 10, 11, 12, 18, 19, 22, 26, 27, 28, 30
silique 4
simple fruit 4
stalk vegetables 13
Star fruit 23
stems 10, 12, 13
stone fruit 4

T
trees 4, 27

U
utricle 4

V
Vitamin A 8, 9, 14, 15, 16, 19, 20
Vitamin C 6, 8, 14, 15, 17, 18, 19, 20
vitamins 5, 6, 8, 12, 13, 14, 15, 17, 20, 21, 22, 30

PEGASUS ENCYCLOPEDIA LIBRARY

Food and Nutrition
NUTRITION

Edited by: Pallabi B. Tomar, Hitesh Iplani
Managing editor: Tapasi De
Designed by: Vijesh Chahal, Anil Kumar, Rohit Kumar
Illustrated by: Suman S. Roy, Tanoy Choudhury
Colouring done by: Vinay Kumar, Kiran Kumari & Pradeep Kumar

NUTRITION

CONTENTS

What is nutrition? 3

History 5

Types of nutrients 7

What is malnutrition? 10

What is plant nutrition? 12

What is animal nutrition? 14

What is human nutrition? 15

What is sports nutrition? 17

Processed foods 19

Why is proper nutrition important? 20

Dangers of poor nutrition 23

Nutrition & life cycles 26

Tips for a healthy diet 29

Test Your Memory 31

Index 32

What is nutrition?

Nutrition is the science that studies the process by which living organisms acquire all the things that are necessary for them to live and grow. Nutrition focuses on the role of nutrients, which are defined as substances that the body cannot make on its own and include things like vitamins, minerals and certain macromolecules. Basically, nutrition consists of diet (what you take in) and metabolism (what happens to it after it enters your body).

Food taken in any form either solid or liquid supplies the body a means to produce energy of any form. The available nutrition in the food promotes growth and maintenance of the body. Proper nutrition is only possible when the diet taken is balanced and the food consumed contains all the basic nutrients.

No single food is rich in all the nutrients so a variety of food should be included to fulfil all the requirements of the body as far as nutrients are concerned. When the food consumed does not fulfil the requirements of nutrients, it leads to malnutrition or under nutrition.

Astonishing fact

Most likely due to poor nutrition as children, many Greeks and Romans were shorter than people today. Men from Pompeii, for example, averaged 5 ft 5½ inches and women averaged 5 ft 2 inches.

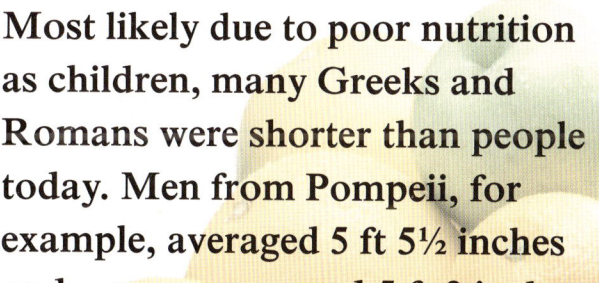

NUTRITION

Good nutrition requires a satisfactory diet, which is capable of supporting the individual consuming it, in a state of good health by providing the desired nutrients in the required amounts. It must provide the right amount of fuel to execute normal physical activity. If the total amount of nutrients provided in the diet is insufficient, a state of under nutrition will develop.

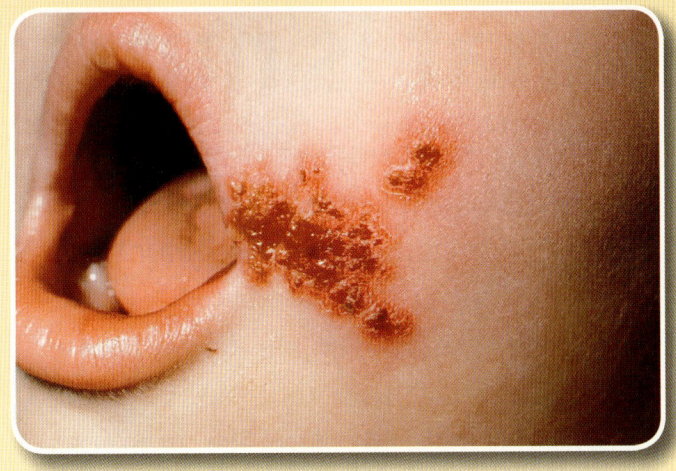

Astonishing fact

The English are sometimes called 'limeys' because British sailors would eat limes to stave off scurvy. Limes were later replaced by lemons due to the lack of adequate vitamin C in lime juice.

Nutrition also focuses on how diseases, conditions and problems can be prevented or lessened with a healthy diet.

Nutrition also involves identifying how certain diseases, conditions or problems maybe caused by dietary factors, such as poor diet (malnutrition), food allergies, metabolic diseases, etc.

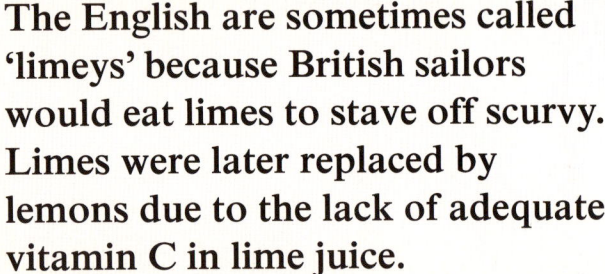

History

The history of the study of food as medicine reveals centuries of discovery and development. Although, modern science and the latest discoveries in biology, medicine and health inform today's field of nutrition and diet, people have been investigating the very real link between food and health since ancient times.

In 400 B.C. the Greek physician Hippocrates said, 'Let thy food be thy medicine and thy medicine be thy food.' Hippocrates realized that food impacts a person's health, body and mind to help prevent illness as well as maintain wellness.

In Hippocrates' Greece, as well as across pre-modern Europe and Asia since ancient times, foods were used to affect health. For instance, Garlic was used to cure athlete's

Dr. James Lind

foot and eating ginger was thought to stimulate the metabolism.

In 1747, a British Navy physician, Dr. James Lind, saw that sailors were developing scurvy, a deadly bleeding disorder, on long voyages. He observed that they ate only non-perishable foods such as bread and meat. Lind's experiment fed one group of sailors' salt water, one group with vinegar and one group limes. Those given limes didn't develop scurvy. And although Vitamin C wasn't discovered until the 1930s, this experiment changed the way physicians thought about food.

Astonishing fact

Vitamin D is unusual because it is the only vitamin that can be synthesized in the body. Sunlight is the main source of Vitamin D.

NUTRITION

During the Enlightenment and into the Victorian age, scientific and medical development increased rapidly. The concept of metabolism, the transfer of food and oxygen into heat and water in the body, creating energy, was discovered in 1770 by Antoine Lavoisier. And in the early 1800s, the importance of the elements of carbon, nitrogen, hydrogen and oxygen the main components of food, were recognised as being essential to health.

In 1912, E.V. McCollum, a US Department of Agriculture researcher at the University of Wisconsin, began using rats instead of humans in his experiments rather than cows and sheep. He found the first fat-soluble vitamin, Vitamin A,

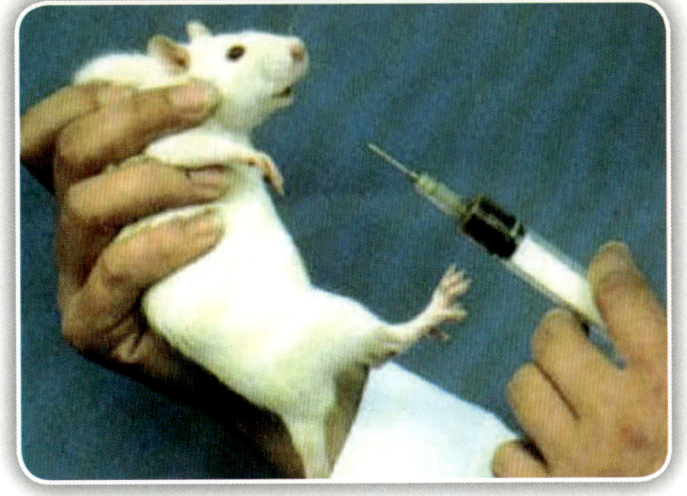

and discovered that rats were healthier when they were fed butter rather than lard, as butter contains more Vitamin A. Other diseases were linked to vitamin deficiencies, such as beri-beri, resulting from a lack of Vitamin B and rickets, brought on by a lack of Vitamin D.

Many other vitamins were discovered and isolated in the early 20th century and the concept of supplementing health with vitamins was born. The first vitamin pills were marketed in the 1930s and created a new industry around science-based health products.

Astonishing fact

The term 'vitamin' was coined by Polish-American chemist Casimir Funk and is derived from vital (necessary for life) and amine (a compound containing nitrogen and hydrogen).

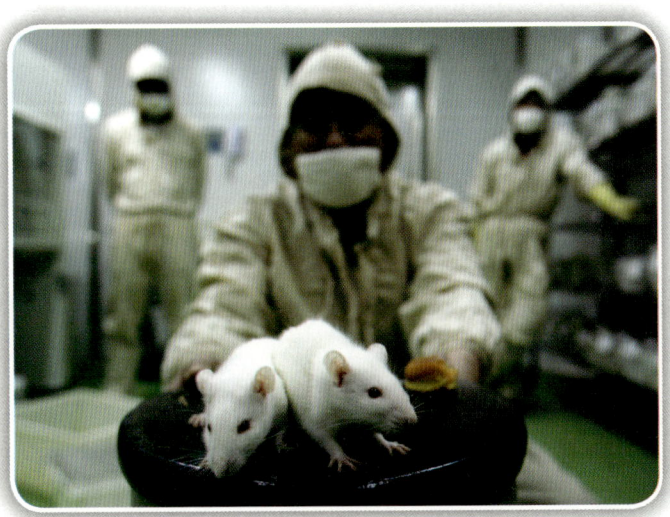

Types of nutrients

The body breaks down the foods we eat in order to use nutrients found in these items. While many people focus on eating healthy foods in order to maintain a healthy weight, not getting the proper nutrients can cause problems beyond weight gain. There are six types of nutrients the body needs to survive.

Rice

Carbohydrates

Carbohydrates are primarily responsible for fuelling your body, giving you energy throughout the day. Some carbohydrates, like table sugar, are broken down very quickly for quick bursts of energy, while other carbohydrates, like whole grains are more complex. Complex carbohydrates take longer to break down and thus fuel you with energy slowly throughout the day. Foods high in carbohydrate include fruits, sweets, soft drinks, breads, pastas, beans, potatoes, bran, rice and cereals.

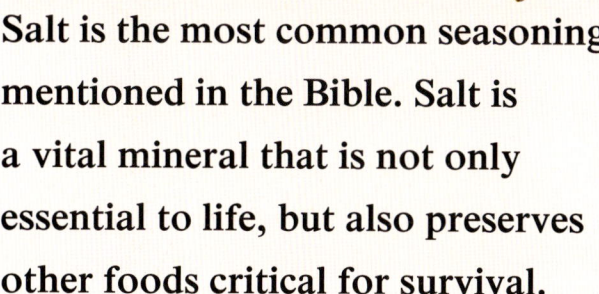

Astonishing fact

Salt is the most common seasoning mentioned in the Bible. Salt is a vital mineral that is not only essential to life, but also preserves other foods critical for survival.

Fats

Fats are our storehouses of energy. When we have excess nutrients in our body, some of it is stored as fat. The primary purpose of fat is energy production. There are two main types of fats—saturated and unsaturated. Animal fats (meat, butter, lard) are usually saturated fats and contribute to heart disease and cancer. Vegetable fats (olive oil, corn oil) are generally unsaturated fats and are less harmful. Some fats have been found to be helpful in preventing some cancers and heart disease. These fats called omega-3 fatty acids are found in some fish, especially cold-water fish.

Fish

Proteins

Proteins provide the body with material to grow. Where carbohydrates and fats are broken down to produce energy, protein is broken down to give your body material for tissue repair and growth. Common protein rich foods can include milk, soy milk, eggs, cheese, yogurt, peanut butter, lean meats, fish and poultry, beans, tofu, lentils and other legumes, grains, including bread and pasta, nuts and seeds.

Astonishing fact

Salt was so important that it was also often used as a form of currency or as a unit of exchange!

Minerals

Minerals are compounds, obtained from your diet, that combine in several ways to form the structures of your body. For instance, calcium is a mineral that is crucial in the formation and maintenance of your bones. Minerals also help regulate body functions. Minerals do not produce energy.

Types of nutrients

Vitamins

Vitamins are substances that your body needs to grow and develop normally. There are 13 vitamins your body needs. They are vitamins A, C, D, E, K and the B vitamins (thiamine, riboflavin, niacin, pantothenic acid, biotin, vitamin B-6, vitamin B-12 and folate). You can usually get all your vitamins from the foods you eat. Your body can also make vitamins D and K.

Each vitamin has specific jobs. If you have low levels of certain vitamins, you may develop a deficiency disease. For example, if you don't get enough vitamin D, you could develop rickets. Some vitamins may help prevent medical problems. Vitamin A prevents night blindness.

Water

Water is, perhaps, the most critical nutrient. We can live without other nutrients for several weeks, but we can go without water for only about a week. The body needs water to carry out all of its life processes. Watery solutions help dissolve other nutrients and carry them to all the tissues. The chemical reactions that turn food into energy or tissue-building materials can take place only in a watery solution. The body also needs water to carry away waste products and to cool itself.

Astonishing fact

Temperature can affect appetite. A cold person is more likely to eat more food.

NUTRITION

What is malnutrition?

Malnutrition occurs when the body does not get enough nutrients. This can mean not getting enough food overall, which can lead to starvation or can be the lack of a single nutrient, such as Vitamin C deficiency, which can lead to scurvy. Causes of malnutrition include not having enough food to eat, not being able to eat a balanced diet, having medical problems that prevent food from being absorbed properly or having psychological problems, such as anorexia nervosa (loss of appetite).

Symptoms of malnutrition vary according to the type of malnutrition and the severity of the problem. If an individual's malnutrition is mild, the person may not show any symptoms at all. General symptoms of this condition can include dizziness, tiredness or weight loss. A person should contact a physician when the individual experiences fainting or hair loss.

The problem is more difficult in areas of widespread poverty or famine. First, there may not be adequate supplies of food. Second, people may not have the money to purchase food that is available. Third, there may not be enough doctors and physicians available to treat not only malnutrition, but any underlying causes beyond lack of food that may be leading to this condition.

Malnutrition is the largest single contributor to disease, according to the UN's Standing Committee on Nutrition (SCN).

> The word 'health' comes from the Anglo-Saxon term 'hal' meaning 'wholeness'.

Astonishing fact

The human digestive system is home to between 10 and 100 trillion bacteria, at least 10 times the amount of cells in the body!

What is malnutrition?

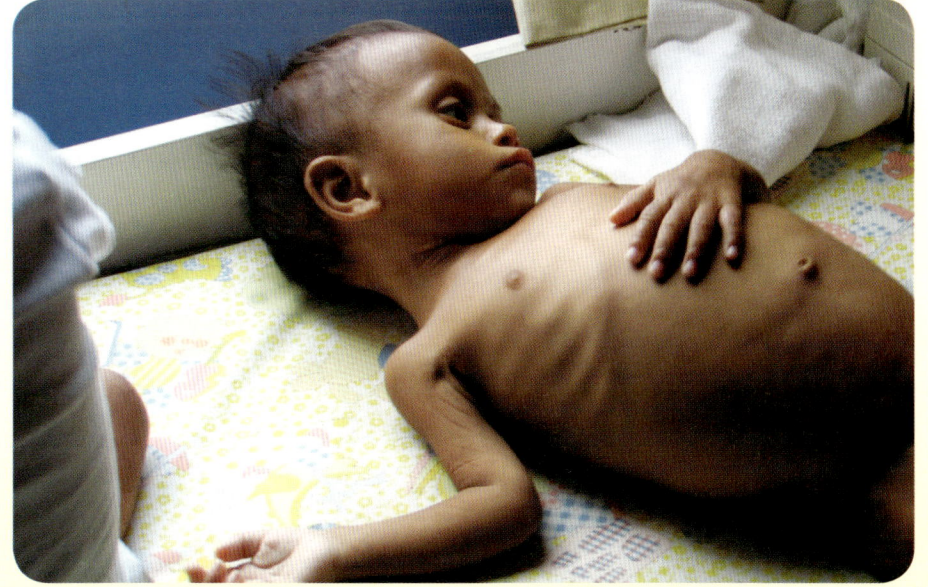

Malnutrition at an early age leads to reduced physical and mental development during childhood. Stunting, for example, affects more than 147 million pre-schoolers in developing countries, according to SCN's World Nutrition Situation 5th report. Iodine deficiency is the world's greatest single cause of mental retardation and brain damage.

Malnutrition can occur because of the lack of a single vitamin in the diet or it can be because a person isn't getting enough food. Starvation is a form of malnutrition. Malnutrition also occurs when adequate nutrients are consumed in the diet, but one or more nutrients are not digested or absorbed properly.

Malnutrition may be mild enough to show no symptoms. However, in some cases it may be so severe that the damage done is irreversible, even though the individual survives.

Worldwide, malnutrition continues to be a significant problem, especially among children who cannot fend adequately for themselves. Poverty, natural disasters, political problems and war, all contribute to conditions, even epidemics of malnutrition and starvation, and not just in developing countries.

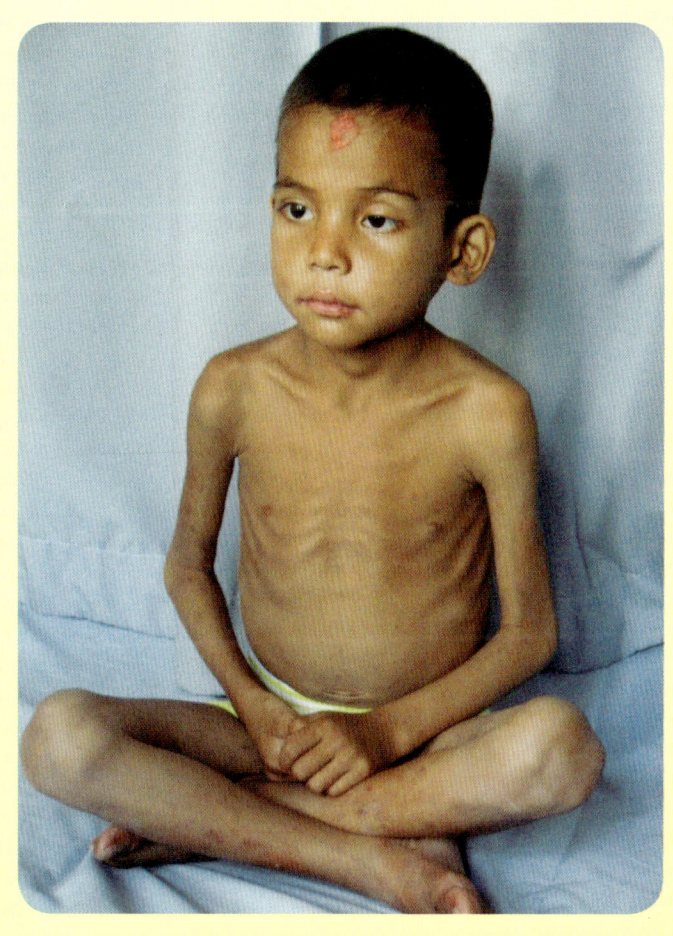

What is plant nutrition?

Plants need 17 elements for normal growth. Carbon, hydrogen, and oxygen are found in air and water. Nitrogen, potassium, magnesium, calcium, phosphorous and sulphur are found in the soil. These six elements are used in relatively large amounts by the plant and are called **macronutrients**. There are eight other elements that are used in much smaller amounts and are called **micronutrients** or trace elements. The micronutrients which are found in the soil are iron, zinc, molybdenum, manganese, boron, copper, cobalt, and chlorine. All 17 elements, both macronutrients and micronutrients are essential for plant growth.

A balanced nutrition program is essential if plants are to grow and yield to their maximum potential. Adequate nutrition will ensure the plants are structurally strong with increased vigour, giving increased resistance to the penetration of fungal organisms and the possibility to organize their defence mechanisms.

An adequate supply of **nitrogen** is important, as it is essential in the formation of amino acids, which are the building blocks for proteins. Conversely, a surplus of nitrogen leads to overly lush growth, with the soft tissue produced being more open to to disease.

What is plant nutrition?

Phosphorus is essential for a multiplicity of plant functions and it can be replaced by no other element. It is involved in photosynthesis, energy transfer and storage, respiration, cell division and cell enlargement. Phosphorus promotes early root formation and growth, it hastens maturity and it contributes to disease resistance in plants.

Potassium is a vital element and again cannot be replaced by anything else. For plants to produce high yields, particularly of fruits, it is probably of greater importance than nitrogen. It is involved in many processes in the plant including photosynthesis and respiration, activating enzymes and controlling reaction rates within the plant. It is important in protein synthesis, ionic balance, cell turgidity and root development, increasing winter hardiness and disease resistance in plants.

Sulphur also plays an important role in plant growth and health. It is essential for chlorophyll formation and aids in the production of enzymes and vitamins, which are vital for vigorous, healthy, plants.

Astonishing fact

A deficiency of calcium/Vitamin D during infancy or childhood results in rickets (deformed bones). The bones can become so weak that they can't withstand the body's weight, causing bow legs or knock knees. Once malformed, bones cannot be straightened.

13

What is animal nutrition?

Animal nutrition incorporates fodder and crop production, fodder conservation, also feed manufacture and the quality control of feeds. Quality of the animal-origin foods is affected mainly by quality of the animal feeds and therefore this latter one has crucial importance in human nutrition.

Animals need a variety of nutrients to meet their basic needs. These nutrients include fats and carbohydrates that provide energy, proteins that furnish amino acids, vitamins that serve as co-factors for enzymes and perform other functions, ions required for water balance and for nerve and muscle function, and selected elements that are incorporated into certain molecules synthesized by cells. To determine the levels of nutrients that are needed to sustain normal activities, researchers monitor the relationship between nutrient intake, the levels of nutrients maintained in the body and health.

Astonishing fact

A person usually swallows around 250 times during dinner.

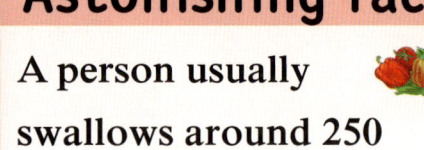

What is human nutrition?

Human nutrition is composed of all the materials in the form of food necessary to support life. A healthy diet plays a crucial role in alleviating some health problems such as obesity, cardiovascular disease, diabetes and metabolic syndrome. It also prevents the onset of such deficiency-related diseases like beriberi, scurvy and kwashiorkor. Nutrients come in six major classes.

Human nutrition is the provision to humans to obtain the materials necessary to support life. In general, humans can survive for two to eight weeks without food, depending on stored body fat.

Astonishing fact

Vitamin B12 deficiency can lead to anaemia, neural disorders and psychotic behaviour.

Survival without water is usually limited to three or four days. Lack of food remains a serious problem, with about 36 million humans starving to death every year. Childhood malnutrition is also common and contributes to the global burden of disease. However, global food distribution is not even and obesity among some human populations has increased to almost epidemic proportions, leading to health complications and increased mortality in some developed and a few developing countries. Obesity is caused by consuming more calories than are expended, with many attributing excessive weight gain to a combination of overeating and insufficient exercise.

15

NUTRITION

Human food contains both vegetables and animals. Both serve in some respects the same purpose in the body, while in others their use is different. Either vegetable or animal food would sustain life, but both together serve much better than either could.

Plant food supplies most of the energy and endurance of the body in starch, sugar and vegetable-oil foods; also much of the body-heat, the food-bulk required for digestive activity, the salts needed for body-regulation, and the water used in living processes and food-utilization. Some vegetable food can also build up body-tissues as it needs repair or material for growth.

The human body contains chemical compounds such as water, carbohydrates, amino acids (in proteins), fatty acids and nucleic acids (DNA and RNA). These compounds in turn consist of elements such as carbon, hydrogen, oxygen, nitrogen, phosphorus, calcium, iron, zinc, magnesium, manganese and so on. All of these chemical compounds and elements occur in various forms and combinations (e.g. hormones, vitamins, phospholipids), both in the human body and in the plant and animal organisms that humans eat.

Astonishing fact

Insects such as termites and ants provide 10 per cent of the protein consumed worldwide. Where insects are an integral part of a diet, they contribute as much as 40 per cent of protein!

What is sports nutrition?

Sports nutrition is a branch of nutritional science which focuses on the unique nutritional needs of athletes. People who want to achieve better athletic performance often need to adjust their diets to meet their physical needs and professional athletes often use the services of an experienced dietician or nutritionist to make sure that their diets are designed appropriately.

Astonishing fact

Some children and pregnant women crave non-nutritive substances such as paint, plaster, rocks and dirt. These cravings may suggest the person lacks certain minerals, such as iron.

Athletes burn a lot of energy, which means that they need to consume more energy than inactive individuals. One of the best sources of energy is carbohydrates, making an increased carbohydrate intake critical for an athlete. Athletes also usually require slightly more protein. They also need the recommended amounts of fruits and vegetables.

Another critical nutritional need for athletes is water consumption. Failure to drink enough water can result in an electrolyte imbalance which can cause medical problems. So, it is important for athletes to integrate water into their dietary plans and to make sure that water is consumed in appropriate amounts at the right intervals, as too much water can also be damaging.

NUTRITION

Different types of athletes have different nutritional needs. Sprinters and marathon runners, for example, require different things from their bodies, and they are also trained differently for races, which mean that their diets will be different. Sports nutrition considers the sport an athlete is involved in and his or her physical condition. Different nutrition may also be involved for training, tapering down after a meet or gearing up for a meet.

Many athletes try to eat food which is healthy, in addition to nutritionally necessary. They may opt for a heavy concentration of fresh foods, for example and try to avoid packaged foods if possible.

Sports clubs and gyms sometimes offer nutrition for sports workshops, which are an excellent resource for information on sports nutrition. Personal trainers can also provide tips and advice, whether people are trying to build muscle for bodybuilding or trim down for rock climbing. Athletes at all levels can also work with nutrition professionals to tailor a diet regimen which will meet their needs, and to learn more about the complex science behind sports nutrition.

Astonishing fact

Improved nutrition has extended the average U.S. lifespan from 30 to 40 years old in the early twentieth century to 70 to 80 years old today.

Processed foods

Food processing is the set of methods and techniques used to transform raw ingredients into food or to transform food into other forms for consumption by humans or animals either in the home or by the food processing industry. Food processing typically takes clean, harvested crops or butchered animal products and uses these to produce attractive, marketable and often long shelf-life food products. Similar processes are used to produce animal feed. The methods used for processing foods include canning, freezing, refrigeration and aseptic processing.

Processed foods usually do not get spoiled soon unlike fresh foods, and are better suited for long distance transportation from the source to the consumer. When they were first introduced some processed foods helped to alleviate food shortages and improved the overall nutrition of populations as it made many new foods available to the masses.

Astonishing fact
Eggs contain the highest quality food protein known. All parts of an egg are edible, including the shell which has high calcium content!

Another healthy example of food processing is frozen vegetables. While fresh maybe best, freezing vegetables preserves vitamins and minerals and makes them convenient to cook and eat all year around. Fruit and vegetable juice is also an example of a healthy processed food. In fact, some orange juice is fortified with calcium to make it even more nutritious.

Of course, there are a lot of processed foods that aren't good for you. Many processed foods are made with Trans fats, saturated fats and large amounts of sodium and sugar. These types of foods should be avoided or at least eaten sparingly.

NUTRITION

Why is proper nutrition important?

Apart from providing you with energy, nutrition also involves an understanding of how a healthy diet prevents the development of diseases, problems and other conditions of the body.

The foods you eat provide the energy your body needs to function. Just like you need to put fuel in your car or recharge your cell phone battery, your body needs to be fed with energy-providing foods every day. The main energy provider of our body is carbohydrates.

Your body has the easiest time digesting carbohydrates like sugar and starch. Carbohydrates are broken down into individual glucose, fructose or galactose units. Glucose is your body's favourite form of energy. If you don't get enough carbohydrates, your body can make glucose from protein or fat and if you get too many carbohydrates, your body is very good at storing them as fat.

Protein in the foods you eat is broken down into individual amino acids. Your body uses the amino acids to build and repair the various parts of your body. Your muscles contain lots of protein and you need to replenish that protein through your diet. Your body also needs protein for components of your immune system, hormones, nervous system and organs.

Another raw material your body needs is calcium. Calcium has several functions in your body, but its best known as the mineral that is stored in your bones and teeth. You need calcium from your diet to keep your bones and teeth strong.

Your body also needs fats to be healthy. Membranes that contain fats surround all the cells of your body. Your brain has fatty acids and fats are also needed to signal hormones.

Why is proper nutrition important?

You need energy to engage in your daily physical and mental activities. Upon digestion, food that you eat is broken into smaller molecules like glucose, amino acids, fats and vitamins. These molecules and nutrients are the elements that provide your energy.

Among the cells present in your body are egg, bones, fat, muscle, brain, nerve and blood cells. All the cells have functions to perform. The body loses cells and makes new ones. Your body tissues are made up of millions of cells. The nutrients that travel through your bloodstream prevent damage, keep these cells alive and help in producing new ones.

Waste and toxic materials from indigestible food burden your body. A healthy diet should contain lots of fresh fruits and vegetables to cleanse and ease the process of eliminating your waste matter.

You have to take good care of your body because it is a vehicle to transport you from one place to another and to enable you to do the things that you dream of doing. The food that you take in is going to help you to complete your tasks and fulfil all your dreams.

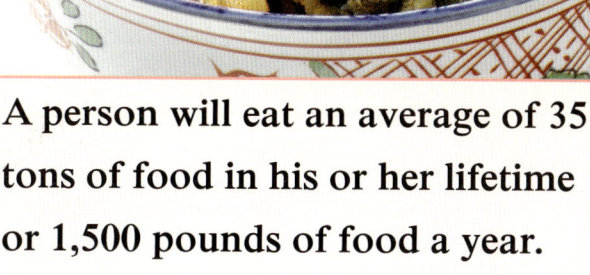

A person will eat an average of 35 tons of food in his or her lifetime or 1,500 pounds of food a year.

21

NUTRITION

Having good nutrition means eating the right types of foods in the right amounts so that you get all the important nutrients. There are no special diets or particular foods that will boost your immune system. But there are things you can do to keep your immunity up. For example if you are underweight or you have advanced disease you should include more protein as well as extra calories in the form of carbohydrates and fats in your diet.

Astonishing fact

Beets are loaded with vitamins A, B1, B2, B6 and C. The greens have a higher content of iron compared to spinach. They are also an excellent source of calcium, magnesium, copper, phosphorus, sodium and iron.

Proper nutrition means getting all the essential nutrients from your diet that is required to keep your body functioning normally. It is important because there are some important molecules that your body uses to live that it cannot make on its own. The essential nutrients must be obtained in the diet or your body will have a shortage of them. This is critical because your body needs the right amount of all the required molecules to function properly. It is like a string of holiday lights that needs every light to be in place and functioning properly in order to light up; if one light is missing, the whole string loses its beauty. In the same way, if you do not have proper nutrition, your body will lack in one or more essential nutrients and will not be able to function normally.

Dangers of poor nutrition

Nutritional disorders can affect anyone, but most commonly plague the elderly and young children. When the diet does not contain the necessary nutrients and vitamins that are required for the proper functioning of the body's systems, problems may occur within the body. Dysfunctions can result from a nutritional deficiency, which can often be remedied once a change in diet or supplementation is initiated.

Rickets

Rickets can result from a severe deficiency of Vitamin D. It can cause the bones to become soft and malleable which can cause developing bones in children to become deformed. A supplement of vitamin or an increase in foods with high Vitamin D content is advised. Foods high in Vitamin D include salmon, milk products and eggs.

Anaemia

Anaemia is a condition in the body where oxygen can't be utilized through the blood as it should, and the organs and muscles in the body become fatigued. This is because the body is not producing an adequate amount of red blood cells. These blood cells are a necessary component because they help the oxygen get to the body's systems. Anaemia is caused by a depletion of iron in the blood and can be the result of poor diet. Increasing foods into the diet that contain high levels of iron, including liver and clams can alleviate anaemia, as can taking an iron supplement.

Astonishing fact

One apple on average contains more antioxidants than a large Vitamin C dose of 1,500 mg.

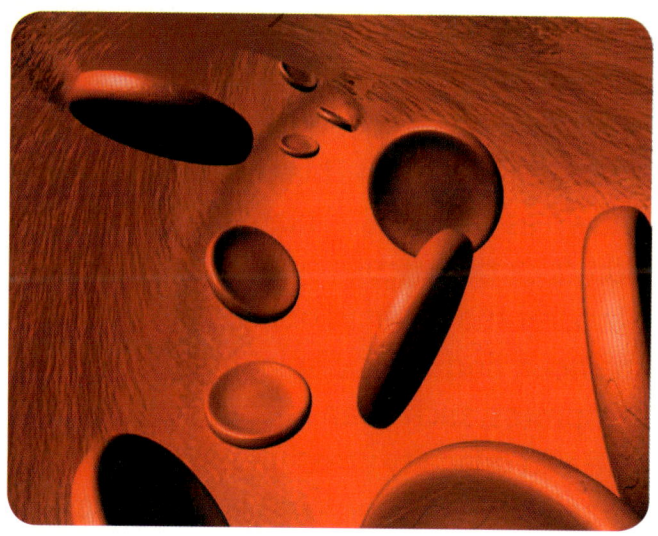

NUTRITION

Scurvy

Scurvy is the result of a vitamin C deficiency. It is becoming more common due to the lack of fresh fruits and vegetables in the modern diet. Scurvy can cause the tissues in the body to disconnect and can lead to severe dental abnormalities and joint problems. To alleviate scurvy, take in more fruits and vegetables into the diet that are high in vitamin C, including oranges, strawberries and bell peppers.

Beriberi

Beriberi occurs in people that have a severe deficiency in Thiamine, otherwise known as vitamin B1. Thiamine helps the body's cardiovascular system function properly and when Beriberi occurs, the heart and lungs display stressed symptoms, such as an increase in heart rate and difficulty breathing. To treat a Thiamine deficiency, include foods into the diet high in vitamin B1, including sunflower seeds, lentils and pinto beans.

Pellagra

Pellagra is a nutritional deficiency that can cause skin disorders in the body, such as dermatitis and psoriasis and mental confusion. It can be the result of eating a diet based heavily on grains, without foods that contain Niacin, such as chicken, beef and salmon. To prevent and alleviate Pellagra, incorporate more meats into the diet.

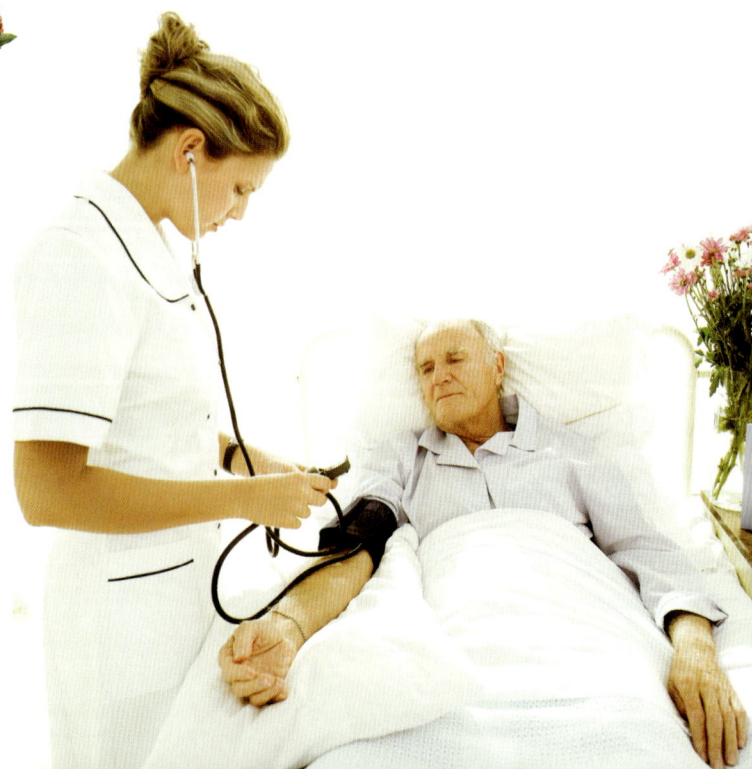

24

Dangers of poor nutrition

Heart diseases

Coronary heart diseases are a very common health problem and they are closely linked to a diet that is high in unhealthy fats. Decreasing one's intake of fatty foods, especially fried food, will go a long way in preventing heart diseases. On the other hand, a healthy diet chart with an adequate amount of high fibre foods is seen to prevent heart diseases. People who suffer from heart problems are often advised to follow a specific high fibre diet for heart diseases that is rich in raw fruits and vegetables.

In addition to these diseases, conditions such as high cholesterol, high blood pressure, gout and even cancer are affected by the individual's diet.

A balanced diet comprising of diverse and healthy foods is key to promoting good health. After all, we are what we eat. Research continues to prove that eating healthy food promotes good health and unhealthy food habits lead to a diseased body. Foods contain vital nutrients that aid our body's metabolic function. However, a lack of consumption of these nutrients or feeding upon the wrong kinds of food leads to an accumulation of toxins within the body, resulting in chronic diseases in the long run.

Diabetes

While genetics does play an important role in the onset of diabetes, an unhealthy lifestyle and bad eating habits are also contributing factors. A diabetes diet chart is a diet plan that is high in fibre and low in fat with a minimum amount of saturated fats.

Astonishing fact

Bananas contain everything a human needs and they contain all the 8 amino-acids our body cannot produce itself.

Nutrition & life cycles

Humans require the same nutrients throughout their lifespan. The amount of specific nutrients varies at different stages in the life cycle and varies according to gender, activity level and growth. Certain health conditions and diseases similarly alter nutritional requirements.

Infants: First Year

Infancy is a period of rapid growth and critical nutrition needs. Infants double their birth weight in six months and triple it in one year.

Other nutritional issues during infancy are switching from breast milk or formula to whole milk and solid food, as well as identifying any food allergies.

Toddlers: 1 to 3 Years

Toddlers prefer sweet and salty as they reject bitter and sour foods. Toddlers may reject a new food 5 to 10 times before accepting it, so frequent tasting helps. Children who eat at the table with adults eat more.

Astonishing fact

Colour also plays a role in the food that we eat. Studies have revealed that warm colours like red, orange and yellow seem to cause us to be hungrier.

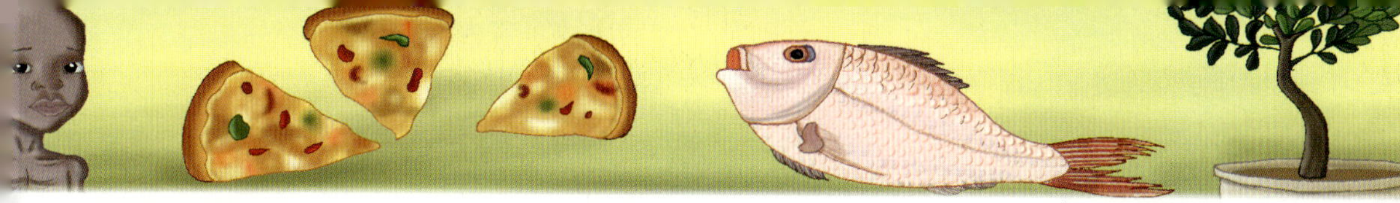

Nutrition & life cycles

Childhood: 3 to 10 Years

Energy needs change with rapid growth spurts and periods of no growth. Calcium, iron, fluoride and fibre are important nutrients at this stage.

Nutritional risk in children is associated with poverty, diet and the knowledge level of parents. Offer children a variety of healthful foods including fruits and vegetables, whole grains, and proteins in child-sized portions and make mealtime pleasant.

Adolescence: 11 to 20 Years

Protein, vitamins and energy needs related to growth rate and activity level are increased. Adequate supplies of Vitamin D, magnesium and protein are also critical for adolescent growth. Calcium needs are greatest during puberty, but drinking less milk and more sweetened beverages may lower calcium intake. Body image, peers and media affect eating behaviours.

27

NUTRITION

Adults: 21 to 65 Years

Physiologic changes, stress, pregnancy and menopause present nutritional challenges in adults. The risk of cancer, heart disease, stroke, diabetes and hypertension can be significantly lowered by modest changes in diet and exercise to reduce weight and change the body composition.

Adequate intake of fruits and vegetables, anti-oxidants, especially Vitamins A and C, whole grains and a reduction in saturated fat, cholesterol, and Trans fats reduces health risks.

Aging: Over 65 Years

Physical changes with aging result in less absorption of calcium, iron, folate, Vitamins B6 and B12 and less efficient production of Vitamin D.

Changes in taste and smell may lead to a decline of appetite and weight loss. A less active body requires fewer calories but more nutrients. The need increases for fibre, fluids and protein.

Vitamins D, B12, A, and E, as well as folate, calcium and magnesium are important nutrients. Increase the intake of fruits and vegetables, whole grains and protein to address these needs.

Astonishing fact

Frozen vegetables can actually be healthier for you than fresh produce, since vegetables lose their nutrients as they wait to be eaten and freezing your vegetables stops that process.

Tips for a healthy diet

Food has undergone many changes as science and technology have progressed and many new aspects of food have been revealed. Nutrition took on a mantle of its own and today forms a very important part in dictating our daily food intake. No longer do most people just eat to live.

Nutrition has been classified into six major nutrition groups namely **carbohydrates**, **proteins**, **fats**, **vitamins**, **minerals** and water. Each one has a role to play in providing a balanced diet to the body.

Each food group has its own part to play in the overall diet of an individual. To avoid stomach disorders and other food related problems, such as indigestion and ulcers, one has to try and eat a balanced meal which contains as many food groups as possible. This is turn will lead to a balanced diet wherein all food ingested is nutritious and can be utilized by the body without any wastage.

Avoid starchy food, fatty foods, foods heavy in spices, and foods with additives wherever possible as these do not aid digestion. Similarly, an excess of salt and sugar would be harmful and the benefits that these foods normally provide would be lost. Every food item plays a small part in our overall nutrition and health. Anything that is too little or too much would upset the balance of the body and its system.

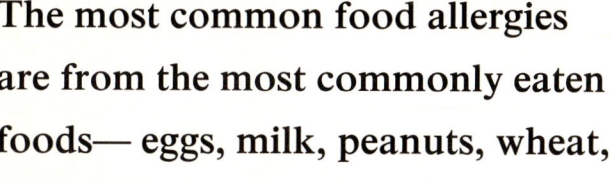

Astonishing fact

The most common food allergies are from the most commonly eaten foods— eggs, milk, peanuts, wheat, fish, and various nuts from trees.

NUTRITION

As with all other fields, food too has seen a lot of innovation and variety. Unfortunately, along with the good food there are also a whole range of foods which has a feel good factor to it but does nothing for the health of the person. These are called **empty calorie foods** in the form of soft drinks, various types of snacks, processed food, etc. Temptation is very difficult to resist so one must strike a balance wherein all desires for food are covered without compromising on the nutrition required by the body.

A good, balanced diet would ideally consist of a controlled intake of saturated and trans fats, cholesterol, sugar and salt, and meats, whilst eating enough fruits, vegetables, wholegrain products, low fat or normal fat dairy products, good fats such as fish, nuts and vegetable oils, fat-free meats, poultry and lentils. Last but not least, check the calorie count of the food on your plate. There is a lot of nutritional information available regarding the content of food and its calorific value. Investing in a guide and eating healthy food could pay rich dividends in future. Along with all this, a sustained and energetic exercise regime will go a long way to a healthy you.

Astonishing fact

Carrots were first cultivated for their medicinal uses and have in recent times been proven to not only improve the health of your eye tissues but your night vision as well.

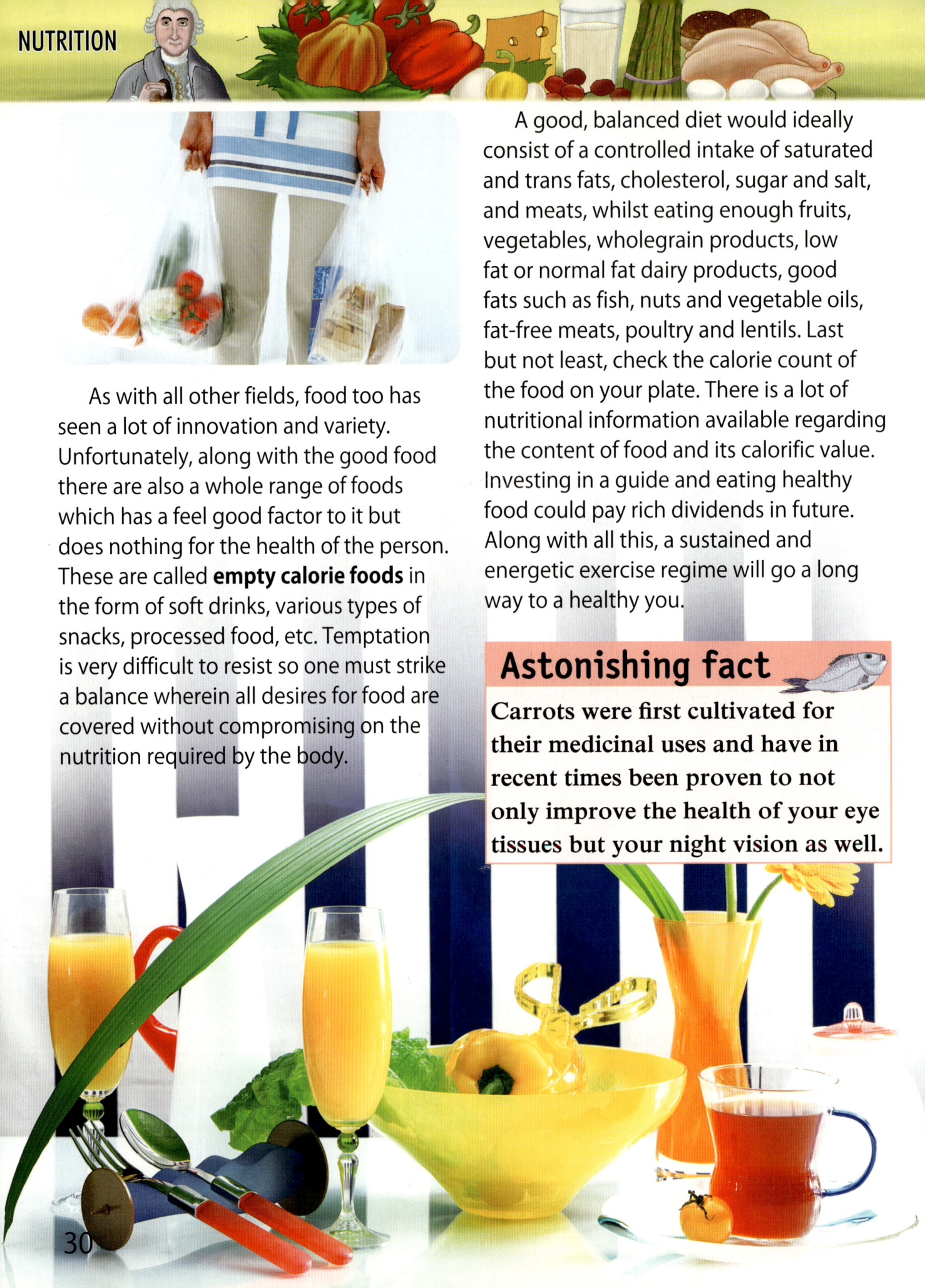

Test Your MEMORY

1. What is nutrition?

2. Write briefly about the history of nutrition.

3. Name the types of nutrients.

4. What is malnutrition?

5. What is plant nutrition?

6. What is animal nutrition?

7. What is human nutrition?

8. What is sports nutrition?

9. What are processed foods?

10. Why is proper nutrition important?

11. What are the dangers of poor nutrition?

12. Write some tips for a healthy diet.

NUTRITION

Index

A
amino acids 12, 14, 16, 20, 21, 25
anaemia 15, 23
Antoine Lavoisier 6
aseptic processing 19

B
beriberi 15, 24

C
calcium 8, 12, 13, 16, 19, 20, 22, 27, 28
calories 15, 22, 28
canning 19
carbohydrates 7, 8, 14, 16, 17, 20, 22, 29

D
diabetes 15, 25, 28
diet 3, 4, 5, 8, 10, 11, 15, 16, 17, 18, 20, 21, 22, 23, 24, 25, 27, 28, 29, 30
dietician 17
dizziness 10
Dr James Lind 5

E
empty calorie foods 30

F
fats 7, 8, 14, 19, 21, 22, 25, 28, 29, 30
fatty acids 7, 16, 20
food allergies 4, 26, 29
food processing 19
freezing 19, 28
fruits 7, 13, 17, 21, 24, 25, 27, 28, 30

G
glucose 20, 21

H
human nutrition 14, 15

I
infants 26

L
limes 4, 5

M
macronutrients 12
magnesium 12, 16, 22, 27, 28
malnutrition 3, 4, 10, 11
metabolism 3, 5, 6
micronutrients 12
minerals 3, 8, 17, 19, 29

N
nitrogen 6, 12, 13, 16
nucleic acids 16
nutrients 3, 4, 7, 9, 10, 11, 14, 15, 21, 22, 23, 25, 26, 27, 28
nutrition 3, 5, 4, 10, 11, 12, 14, 15, 17, 18, 19, 20, 22, 26, 29, 30
nutritional science 17
nutritionist 17

O
obesity 15

P
Pellagra 24
phosphorous 12
plant nutrition 12
potassium 12, 13
proteins 8, 12, 14, 16, 27, 29

R
red blood cells 23
refrigeration 19
rickets 6, 9, 13, 23

S
scurvy 4, 5, 10, 15, 24
sports nutrition 17, 18
starvation 10, 11
sulphur 12, 13

T
toddlers 26

V
vegetables 16, 17, 19, 21, 24, 25, 27, 28, 30
Vitamin A 6, 9
Vitamin B 6
Vitamin D 5, 6, 9, 13, 23, 27, 28
vitamin pills 6
vitamins 3, 6, 9, 13, 14, 16, 19, 21, 22, 23, 27, 28, 29

W
water 6, 9, 12, 14, 15, 16, 17, 29